THE SUPPRESSION T.A.X. Wasted Tears Wasted Taxes

by

Alander Pulliam

THE SUPRESSION T.A.X. WASTED TEARS WASTED TAXES

First edition. November 10, 2025.

ISBN: 979-8232946319

Written by Alander Pulliam.

Table of Contents

Dedication

Dedication: For the Least of These and The Prophets of Now

To the children of the *misguided* who only knew the law as the car that took their parent away. **To the *poor*** whose worth was instantly discounted the moment they stood before the bench without counsel. **To the *oppressed***—the Black, the Brown, the disabled, the divergent—who faced a thousand micro-tyrannies before they ever saw a courthouse.

This is for the spirit that cries out from the abyss of systemic neglect. We dedicate this work to every person who has ever looked at a courtroom or a police car and saw not a promise of protection, but a looming threat—a tax-funded instrument of their personal Gethsemane.

We dedicate this book to the spirit of **prophetic rage**—the kind that overturns the tables of the money-changers in the temple and calls out the hypocrites who love their status more than their sacred duty. And we dedicate it to the spirit of **unconditional love and radical empathy**, which teaches us that the pursuit of justice for *one* is the pursuit of salvation for *all*.

May our words be a balm to your wounds, a shield against the next assault, and a burning coal of conviction in the hearts of those who must now change. **Let the people say Amen. Let the people say *No More*.**

Dedication

A Prophet's Warning to the King-Judge

I. The Heart of Stone: "*For what shall it profit a man, if he shall gain the whole world, and lose his own soul?*" — **Mark 8:36 (KJV, adapted for the Bench)**

II. The Tyranny Tax Defined: "Woe unto you, judges, for you have taken away the key of knowledge: ye entered not in yourselves, and them that were entering in ye hindered. You have mandated that the very citizens you terrorize must fill the public coffers to fund their own shackles. This is the **$UPPRESSION T.A.X.**, and the Lord despises a balance sheet marked with human tears."

III. The Call to Justice with Love: "*He hath shewed thee, O man, what is good; and what doth the Lord require of thee, but to do justly, and to love mercy, and to walk humbly with thy God?* When the law divorces mercy, it becomes a ritual of cruelty. When the officer acts from the heart's anger rather than the mind's duty, he transforms the badge into a **sledgehammer of ego**. This cycle is not sustainable. The people have been silent for too long, but the **Day of Accounting is well overdue.**"

— **Alander Pulliam**, *The New Covenant for the American Citizen*

Front Matter

This document is not a book; it is a **Scroll of Indictment**, delivered from the hands of the oppressed and sealed with the sacred blood of the taxpayer.

For centuries, you have been robbed—not by masked bandits, but by the very institutions sworn to protect you. The ultimate heist is the **$UPPRESSION T.A.X.**, the mandatory levy you pay to fund your own incarceration, your own degradation, and the systemic silencing of your just complaints. You, the working poor, the marginalized citizen, the misguided soul caught in the machine's gears, have been forced to become the unwitting financier of your own oppression.

We declare today that the covenant is broken. The **American Justice System**, cloaked in the majesty of law, has devolved into a cold-hearted **American Business Model**, where profits are measured in fines, fees, and wasted human potential. The system, like a spiritual parasite, feeds on the vulnerabilities of the working class and the easy targets among the disenfranchised, turning the uniform and the robe into **weapons of class and racial warfare.**

We demand an immediate spiritual and political audit. We must confront the **King-Judge**, whose personal ego is his only constitutional amendment, and the **Badge-Bearer**, who mistakes limited public authority for unlimited personal vengeance. Their power, devoid of the saving grace of empathy and the foundational structure of love, is not justice, it is mere tyranny with a taxpayer receipt.

This is the **Malcolm X** moment of fierce, uncompromising truth, coupled with the **Jesus** imperative of radical, transformative compassion. We do not just expose the rotten foundation; we provide the blueprint for the new temple. This is a battle for the soul of the Republic, and it will be fought not with violence, but with procedure, documentation, uncompromising dignity, and the **ferocious love of truth.**

Rise up, you are weary and taxed. Stop funding the tools of your destruction. Your moment to reclaim sovereignty, with both righteous anger and unshakable grace, is well overdue.

Chapter 1: The Price of Silence

The polished mahogany of the courtroom, the solemn pronouncements of judges, the very air thick with the scent of justice – these are the idealized images that linger in the public consciousness. Yet, beneath this veneer of impartiality, a darker reality festers. The American court system, ostensibly a bastion of fairness, has, in many ways, transformed into a labyrinthine engine of extraction, a gilded cage where justice is not dispensed but bartered, and where the scales are tipped not by truth, but by a relentless pursuit of revenue. This isn't the overt corruption of a bribe in the dark alley; it's a systemic, insidious perversion, woven into the very fabric of legal procedure, turning courts into profit centers that prey on the vulnerable and ensnare them in a web of debt.

Consider the seemingly innocuous concept of court fees and fines. On the surface, they appear as legitimate costs associated with the administration of justice, a way to offset the expenses of running the courts. But for the millions caught in the gears of the justice system, particularly those already struggling at the margins of society, these fees morph into a crushing burden, a regressive tax on poverty. A minor traffic infraction, a misdemeanor charge that might seem trivial to some, can, for the indigent, trigger a cascade of financial penalties. Fines are levied, often with little regard for the defendant's ability to pay. When payment is impossible, the debt accrues, compounded by late fees, administrative charges, and collections costs. This isn't justice; it's usury masquerading as law. The debtor's prison, a specter from a bygone era, finds a chilling modern echo in the cycle of warrants, license suspensions, and even jail time that can result from an inability to satisfy these court-imposed financial obligations.

The implications are devastatingly clear: the poor are penalized not just for alleged offenses, but for their poverty itself. A broken taillight, a missed court date due to unreliable public transportation, an inability to afford a lawyer to navigate the complex paperwork – these are not acts of defiance, but the inevitable consequences of economic precarity. Yet, the system often treats them as such, translating these hardships into further financial penalties. Imagine a single mother, working two minimum-wage jobs, struggling to keep food on the table and a roof over her children's heads. A speeding ticket, a few hundred dollars, becomes an insurmountable obstacle. Failure to pay doesn't lead to a discussion about her financial realities; it leads to a warrant. That warrant can result in her arrest, potentially costing her those precious jobs, leaving her children without care, and deepening her entanglement with the very system designed to protect. Her original infraction, however minor, becomes a gateway to a more profound and destructive legal and financial crisis.

This transformation of courts into revenue-generating entities creates a fundamental conflict of interest that gnaws at the heart of judicial integrity. When the financial health of a court system, or indeed the budgetary needs of a municipality, become intertwined with the imposition and collection of fines and fees, the pursuit of justice becomes secondary to the pursuit of revenue. Judges, prosecutors, and court clerks, however well-intentioned they may be individually, operate within a framework that incentivizes punitive financial outcomes. The pressure to meet collection targets, to generate income for local governments, can subtly, or not so subtly, influence decisions. A plea bargain might be encouraged not because it represents a fair resolution, but because it quickly resolves a case and secures a fine. A harsh sentence might be imposed, not because it's proportionate to the offense, but because it carries the potential for future financial penalties through probation fees or restitution that may never be fully paid but serve as ongoing leverage.

The sheer volume of these financial penalties is staggering. Across the nation, countless individuals are trapped in a revolving door of debt, their lives dictated by the relentless pursuit of court-ordered payments. These aren't just abstract numbers; they represent lost opportunities, broken families, and extinguished dreams. A criminal record, often a consequence of an inability to pay fines, can serve as a permanent barrier to employment, housing, and educational advancement. The system, in its relentless pursuit of financial gain, effectively creates a permanent underclass, a segment of society perpetually marginalized and disenfranchised. The court fees and fines become a tool of social control, a mechanism for managing and profiting from poverty, rather than a means of achieving genuine public safety or restorative justice.

The concept of "user fees" within the justice system is particularly insidious. These fees can range from the cost of a court-appointed attorney (even if that attorney's representation is inadequate), to the price of probation supervision, to the cost of electronic monitoring. Essentially, individuals are being charged for the services that are supposed to be their right, or for the mechanisms of their punishment. Imagine being charged by the hour for the privilege of being under surveillance, or paying a daily fee to wear a GPS ankle monitor that restricts your movement and employability. This is not rehabilitation; it's a form of indentured servitude, where the costs of one's own punishment are passed on to the offender, often in perpetuity. For those who cannot pay, the penalties escalate: warrants are issued, leading to arrests, further court costs, and the potential for jail time, all of which generate more fees. The system becomes a self-perpetuating financial cycle, designed not to resolve a transgression, but to extract maximum financial value from the accused.

This financialization of justice has a corrosive effect on public trust. When citizens perceive their courts not as impartial arbiters of truth, but as collection agencies, their faith in the rule of law erodes. The very institutions meant to uphold fairness and equality become viewed with suspicion and resentment. This is particularly true in communities that are disproportionately impacted by these practices – often low-income neighborhoods and communities of color, already bearing the brunt of aggressive policing and systemic discrimination. For these communities, the court system can feel less like a pathway to justice and more like an elaborate trap, designed to ensnare and exploit. The fines and fees, often levied for minor offenses that might be overlooked or handled with greater leniency in more affluent areas, become a constant reminder of their precarious position within the legal and economic hierarchy.

The narrative of justice is often framed around guilt and innocence, punishment and rehabilitation. But the reality, as revealed in the gilded cage of revenue-generating courts, is far more complex and far more predatory. It's about the constant, often unacknowledged, pressure to generate income, a pressure that can warp the fundamental principles of fairness. The justice system, when viewed through this lens, is not an altruistic pursuit of societal well-being, but a complex financial ecosystem. And in this ecosystem, the most vulnerable are not protected; they are harvested. The price of silence, in this context, is not just the absence of a voice, but the accumulation of unpayable debts, the erosion of dignity, and the perpetuation of a cycle of disadvantage that can span generations. The glitter of the courthouse, the solemnity of the proceedings, all serve to mask a deeply ingrained financial imperative that prioritizes profit over people, transforming the pursuit of justice into a ruthless business model. The system, designed to be a shield, becomes a sword, wielded not always with malice, but with a cold, financial logic that leaves its targets bleeding.

The insidious nature of this financialization is further amplified by the lack of transparency. The intricate web of fees, surcharges, and administrative costs associated with court proceedings is often opaque, even to those directly involved. Defendants are rarely presented with a clear, itemized bill of their legal costs upfront. Instead, the penalties accrue, often through a series of notices and demands that can be confusing and intimidating. This lack of clarity allows the system to operate with a degree of plausible deniability, making it difficult to challenge the legitimacy of the charges. It becomes a bureaucratic maze, designed to overwhelm and discourage any attempts at resistance.

Furthermore, the revenue generated from court fees and fines doesn't always directly fund the courts themselves. In many jurisdictions, these funds are diverted to other municipal departments, such as law enforcement or public works. This creates an even more direct incentive for these departments to contribute to the system's revenue stream. Police departments, for instance, may find themselves implicitly tasked with generating arrests that will lead to fines and fees, shifting their focus from community service to revenue generation. This creates a dangerous feedback loop where law enforcement becomes intertwined with the financial objectives of the court system, blurring the lines between public safety and fiscal policy. The very individuals tasked with upholding the law can find themselves acting as agents of extraction, driven by the financial targets embedded within the system.

The impact on due process is profound. When a defendant is overwhelmed by a mountain of debt, their ability to mount a vigorous defense is severely compromised. The fear of escalating financial penalties, of further entanglement with the system, can pressure individuals into accepting plea deals, regardless of their actual guilt or innocence. The complexity of navigating the fee structures, coupled with the threat of further legal action for non-payment, can paralyze a defendant, making it virtually impossible to assert their rights effectively. The right to a fair trial, to adequate legal representation, becomes a hollow promise when the underlying economic realities create such an insurmountable barrier to justice. The "tyranny tax," as it manifests through court fees and fines, doesn't just extract money; it extracts agency, silences voices, and ultimately, perverts the very meaning of justice. It creates a system where financial solvency, rather than factual guilt, can become the determining factor in one's legal fate. This is not a system designed for justice; it is a system designed for extraction, and its success is measured not in acquittals or exonerations, but in the steady flow of revenue extracted from those least able to afford it. The gilded cage is indeed built on a foundation of debt, and its bars are forged from the desperation of the poor.

The siren's wail, a familiar sound in the urban soundscape, is often perceived as a herald of safety, a promise of intervention when danger looms. But what if that siren's song is also the overture to a financial transaction? What if the flashing blue lights, meant to illuminate danger, are also designed to spotlight a potential revenue stream? This is the chilling reality that pervades many American communities, where law enforcement, ostensibly tasked with protecting and serving, has, in practice, become deeply enmeshed in a system that incentivizes profit over genuine public safety. The very institutions designed to uphold the law are, paradoxically, often driven by the pursuit of monetary gain, transforming policing from a service into a business.

The insidious creep of corporatization into public services has not spared the badge. Across the nation, police departments, facing budget constraints and under pressure to demonstrate efficacy in quantifiable terms, have increasingly adopted metrics and practices that mirror those of private enterprise. This is most alarmingly evident in the implementation of what are, in effect, unacknowledged arrest quotas. While departments may officially deny their existence, the pressure on officers to make a certain number of arrests, issue a specific volume of citations, or conduct a predetermined number of traffic stops is palpable. Performance reviews, promotions, and even the allocation of departmental resources can become subtly, or overtly, linked to these numbers. An officer who consistently falls short of these informal targets may find themselves sidelined, their career prospects dimmed, regardless of their community engagement or successful de-escalation efforts.

This quota system creates a dangerous incentive structure. The focus shifts from addressing the root causes of crime or fostering community trust to simply generating quantifiable "outputs." Minor infractions, often those most easily identifiable and prosecutable, become prime targets. A routine traffic stop, which under ideal circumstances might involve a warning or a brief check for safety equipment, can be twisted into an opportunity for a more significant enforcement action. The officer, under implicit pressure, may scrutinize every detail, searching for any deviation from the norm that can be translated into a ticket or an arrest. This proactive search for offenses, rather than a reactive response to observed wrongdoing, can lead to an escalation of minor incidents and a pervasive sense of being under constant surveillance.

The impact of this pressure is felt most acutely in marginalized communities, which often bear the brunt of aggressive policing. These neighborhoods, already grappling with socio-economic disadvantages and a history of strained relations with law enforcement, become fertile ground for revenue-generating policing. Patrols are concentrated in these areas, not necessarily due to a higher incidence of serious crime, but because the potential for issuing citations and making arrests is statistically higher. This creates a feedback loop: increased police presence leads to more minor offenses being detected and punished, which in turn generates more revenue, justifying further intensified policing in those same communities. The message sent to residents is not one of protection, but of perpetual scrutiny and potential penalty.

Beyond arrests and citations, a far more potent and controversial revenue stream for law enforcement lies in asset forfeiture laws. These laws, often enacted under the guise of combating drug trafficking and organized crime, allow police to seize assets suspected of being involved in criminal activity, even if the owner is never convicted of a crime. This is where the lines between law enforcement and financial acquisition become incredibly blurred. Assets ranging from cash and vehicles to homes and businesses can be confiscated, and critically, a significant portion of the proceeds from the sale of these forfeited assets often reverts directly back to the seizing law enforcement agency.

This creates a direct financial incentive for police to pursue asset forfeiture. The prospect of obtaining vehicles for their fleet, upgrading equipment, or even funding departmental initiatives through the sale of confiscated property can influence operational priorities. An officer on patrol, encountering a vehicle that might be associated with a minor drug offense or even a traffic violation that raises suspicion, may be motivated not just by the desire to enforce the law, but by the potential financial windfall that seizing that vehicle could bring. This can lead to disproportionate enforcement actions, where the severity of the alleged offense is secondary to the perceived value of the asset being targeted.

The legal framework surrounding asset forfeiture is notoriously problematic. The burden of proof often falls on the claimant to prove their assets were *not* involved in criminal activity, a difficult and expensive undertaking. Without a criminal conviction, the process can feel like a punishment in itself, a financial drain that can cripple individuals and families. For those operating on the fringes of the economy, or engaged in low-level illicit activities, the loss of a vehicle or a small sum of cash can have devastating consequences, far outweighing the actual harm caused by the underlying offense.

Consider the case of a low-level drug courier, caught with a small amount of narcotics and a modest sum of cash. In a system where asset forfeiture is a significant revenue source, the focus can easily shift from the relatively minor drug offense to the confiscation of the cash, and potentially the vehicle used for transportation. The police department, eager to generate revenue, may prioritize the forfeiture proceedings, even if a conviction for the drug charge is uncertain. The asset becomes the primary target, and the individual's rights can be secondary to the department's financial goals.

This creates a perverse situation where law enforcement agencies can become financially dependent on the very activities they are meant to police. When the seizure and sale of property become a substantial part of a department's budget, there is an inherent conflict of interest. The pursuit of justice can be undermined by the pursuit of profit. Officers may feel compelled to make seizures, even in ambiguous cases, to meet departmental revenue targets. This can lead to overzealous policing, questionable seizures, and a disregard for the due process rights of individuals who are presumed innocent until proven guilty.

The sale of confiscated property further exacerbates this financial entanglement. Police departments often auction off seized vehicles, electronics, and other goods, generating direct income. This creates a marketplace driven by the enforcement of laws, where the profits of the state are derived from the confiscation of private property. The effectiveness of these auctions, and the prices they command, can become a metric of departmental success, further incentivizing aggressive seizure tactics. It transforms officers from public servants into de facto auctioneers, their daily activities indirectly contributing to the department's financial solvency.

The cumulative effect of these profit-driven policing practices is a corrosive erosion of trust between law enforcement and the communities they serve. When residents perceive their police force as primarily concerned with generating revenue, rather than ensuring safety and upholding justice, the foundational relationship of trust crumbles. This is particularly damaging in communities already experiencing high levels of policing and a history of systemic discrimination. The blue lights, instead of signifying protection, begin to represent a threat – a financial threat. The red flags, once signals of danger, become warnings of impending financial penalty.

This creates an atmosphere of fear and resentment. Citizens may become hesitant to report crimes, fearing that their own interactions with the police could lead to financial entanglements. They may view traffic stops not as safety checks, but as potential income-generating opportunities for the officers. This alienation makes community policing initiatives far more difficult to implement effectively. How can officers build rapport and collaborate with residents when the underlying dynamic is one of mutual suspicion and perceived financial exploitation?

The justification often offered for these practices is that the revenue generated funds essential police services, such as new equipment, training, or salary increases. However, this argument masks a fundamental flaw: it places the financial needs of the institution above the principles of justice and the well-being of the community. It suggests that public safety is a commodity that can be bought and sold, with the citizens themselves bearing the cost through fines, fees, and asset seizures. This is not a sustainable or just model for public safety. It creates a system where the vulnerable are disproportionately targeted, and where the pursuit of profit can outweigh the pursuit of true justice.

The emphasis on arrests and seizures as performance indicators also distorts the very definition of effective policing. True public safety is not merely a matter of statistical output; it involves de-escalation, community engagement, problem-solving, and addressing the root causes of crime. When officers are incentivized to make arrests, they may opt for more aggressive tactics, potentially escalating minor situations and leading to unnecessary confrontations. This can result in higher rates of force, increased complaints against officers, and a decline in the overall quality of life in heavily policed communities. The focus on "making cases" can overshadow the more nuanced, yet ultimately more effective, approaches to crime prevention and resolution.

Furthermore, the reliance on fines and asset forfeiture revenue can create a fiscal dependency that makes systemic reform difficult. As departments become accustomed to this influx of cash, any proposal to curb these practices may be met with resistance, as it threatens their operational budgets. This creates a vested interest in maintaining the status quo, even when its negative consequences are evident. The cycle of profit-driven policing becomes self-perpetuating, entrenched by financial necessity and institutional inertia.

The narrative of law enforcement must shift from one of revenue generation to one of service and protection. This requires a fundamental re-evaluation of how police departments are funded and how their performance is measured. Moving away from quota-like systems and profit-incentivized seizures is paramount. Instead, departments should be evaluated on metrics that reflect genuine community safety and trust, such as crime reduction rates achieved through community engagement, successful de-escalation of volatile situations, and a decrease in citizen complaints.

The chilling reality of blue lights and red flags, when viewed through the lens of policing for profit, reveals a system that has strayed from its core mission. It is a system where the pursuit of financial gain can eclipse the ideals of justice, creating a corrosive cycle of distrust and exploitation. To reclaim the promise of public safety, we must dismantle these profit-driven incentives and recommit to a model of policing that is rooted in empathy, accountability, and a genuine dedication to the well-being of all citizens, not just their financial contribution to the system. The siren's call should be one of hope, not a harbinger of financial dread.

The halls of power, gleaming marble and hushed corridors, are not as impervious to the clamor of special interests as they might appear. Behind the carefully constructed facade of legislative deliberation, an unseen hand often guides the pen that signs bills into law. This is the realm of lobbying, a sophisticated and often opaque ecosystem where influence is bought, policy is shaped, and the gears of justice can be deliberately, and profitably, ground. While the public square buzzes with debates about crime rates and public safety, the real legislative heavy lifting—the strategic maneuvering, the backroom deals, the crafted narratives—often occurs far from the spotlight. This subsection delves into the heart of that influence, exposing how private interests, particularly those deeply embedded in the carceral state, have skillfully manipulated the legislative process to ensure their own prosperity, often at the expense of justice and the public good.

Consider the burgeoning private prison industry. These corporations, driven by the imperative to maximize shareholder returns, do not operate on the principle of rehabilitation or public service. Their business model hinges on occupancy rates. The more bodies behind bars, the more revenue flows into their coffers. This stark financial reality necessitates a constant, if not expanding, demand for incarceration. To achieve this, these entities employ armies of lobbyists, well-versed in the art of persuasion and armed with substantial campaign contributions. Their objective is singular: to advocate for tougher sentencing laws, mandatory minimums, and policies that increase the likelihood of imprisonment, regardless of whether such measures genuinely enhance public safety or serve the interests of justice. They are not advocating for a safer society; they are advocating for a fuller prison.

These lobbyists operate with a chilling pragmatism. They meticulously study legislative calendars, identify vulnerable lawmakers, and craft compelling, albeit often misleading, arguments. They might present data on crime statistics that selectively highlight increases, while downplaying decreases or ignoring broader societal factors. They fund think tanks that produce reports echoing their desired policy outcomes, creating an echo chamber of "expert" opinion. They sponsor "awareness campaigns" that tap into public anxieties about crime, framing harsher penalties as the only effective solution. The language they employ is designed to resonate with a public seeking security, masking the underlying profit motive with appeals to law and order. The result is a gradual, insidious capture of the legislative agenda, where policies are enacted not based on their effectiveness or fairness, but on their capacity to generate demand for correctional facilities. This isn't merely advocacy; it's legislative warfare waged with financial artillery, where public policy becomes a casualty.

The influence extends beyond just prison corporations. Law enforcement unions, while often championing the safety and well-being of their members, also wield significant lobbying power. Their priorities, too, can inadvertently, or sometimes deliberately, align with policies that increase the number of arrests and prosecutions. Historically, strong police unions have advocated for expanded police powers, reduced oversight, and policies that make it easier to secure convictions. While some of these aims may stem from a genuine desire for officers to be effective in their duties, they can also translate into legislative support for practices that contribute to mass incarceration. For instance, a union might lobby against reforms that reduce mandatory minimum sentences, arguing that such changes tie officers' hands and make their jobs more dangerous. Or they might push for legislation that expands the scope of offenses for which arrests can be made, or that grants law enforcement more discretion in initiating investigations.

The financial muscle behind these lobbying efforts is substantial. Campaign contributions, "donations" to political action committees (PACs), and the funding of extensive advertising campaigns are all part of the arsenal. This financial leverage allows these special interests to gain access to lawmakers that ordinary citizens can only dream of. Meetings are granted, proposals are considered, and legislation is often drafted with input from these powerful groups. It is a quid pro quo system, where access and consideration are exchanged for financial support or political endorsement. The effect is a gradual poisoning of the legislative well, where the purest intentions of public service can become tainted by the pervasive influence of private gain.

The concept of "legislative capture" is not merely an academic term; it is a lived reality that shapes the laws that govern millions. It describes a situation where a regulatory agency or legislative body, created to act in the public interest, instead advances the commercial or political concerns of specific interest groups that dominate the industry or sector it is charged with regulating. In the context of the justice system, this means that laws are not crafted with the goal of fostering rehabilitation, reducing recidivism, or promoting genuine public safety. Instead, they are sculpted to maintain and expand the flow of individuals into the carceral system. Think of it as a sophisticated industrial complex, where the raw material is human lives, and the product is incarceration. The lobbyists and their corporate patrons are the architects, ensuring a steady supply of that raw material by manipulating the very laws that are supposed to protect society.

This legislative capture manifests in myriad ways. It can be seen in the proliferation of "truth in sentencing" laws, which mandate that offenders serve a substantial portion of their sentence, severely limiting parole and early release opportunities. While ostensibly aimed at ensuring accountability, these laws often lead to overcrowded prisons and do little to address the underlying causes of crime. They are a boon to private prison companies, guaranteeing long-term occupancy. Similarly, the expansion of drug offenses and the imposition of mandatory minimum sentences for even minor drug-related activities, regardless of an individual's role or history, are often the direct result of lobbying efforts. These policies, frequently portrayed as tough on crime, disproportionately impact marginalized communities and contribute to the ever-growing prison population, all while filling the coffers of those who profit from incarceration.

The systemic nature of this oppression is deeply concerning. It is not the work of a few rogue actors, but a carefully orchestrated strategy embedded within the very fabric of our political and legal systems. The "unseen hand" is a vast network of interconnected interests, all working in concert to maintain a status quo that is immensely profitable for them. They benefit from the cycle of arrest, prosecution, and incarceration. They benefit from the fines and fees that are levied, which in turn fund police departments and court systems. They benefit from the steady stream of individuals entering the system, many of whom emerge with shattered lives and limited prospects, perpetuating a cycle of disadvantage that makes them more likely to re-enter the system.

The danger lies in the subtlety of it all. The legislative process can be glacially slow, with changes often occurring incrementally. A single bill might seem innocuous, a minor adjustment here or there. But over years and decades, these small shifts accumulate, like grains of sand building a mountain, creating a legal landscape that is increasingly punitive and less conducive to justice. The public, often distracted by sensational headlines and the immediate anxieties of crime, rarely sees the painstaking, behind-the-scenes work of lobbyists and special interests. They do not witness the quiet conversations, the crafted amendments, the strategic alliances that ultimately determine the fate of legislation and, by extension, the lives of countless individuals.

Furthermore, the influence of these powerful entities can stifle genuine reform efforts. When proposals emerge that aim to reduce reliance on incarceration, promote rehabilitation, or address the root causes of crime, they often face a formidable wall of opposition. This opposition is not always overt; it can manifest as underfunding of alternative programs, the introduction of counter-legislation, or the strategic deployment of fear-based rhetoric. The very institutions designed to create a more just society become obstacles to that goal, ensnared by the profit motive and the vested interests of those who benefit from the current system. The legislative process, intended to be a vehicle for positive change, can become a tool for perpetuating systemic oppression, all under the guise of public safety and law and order. The "unseen hand" is not just guiding the pen; it is actively rigging the game.

The gleaming towers of finance and the hallowed halls of legislation, though seemingly detached from the gritty realities of everyday life, cast long, suffocating shadows over communities across the nation. The abstract machinations of lobbying and legislative capture, the quiet deals struck in dimly lit rooms, translate into a brutal, tangible reality for those living in the crosshairs of an ever-expanding carceral state. This is not a theoretical debate; it is the systematic dismantling of families, the evisceration of economic opportunity, and the erosion of hope in neighborhoods already struggling against systemic disadvantages. The influence peddled from the highest echelons of power doesn't merely shape policy; it dictates the very rhythm of life and death in marginalized communities, turning them into fertile ground for an industry that thrives on their despair.

Consider the relentless tide of aggressive policing, a tactic often justified by the need to "reduce crime," but which in practice acts as a dragnet, sweeping up individuals and ensnaring entire neighborhoods in a web of citations and arrests. These aren't always for heinous offenses. More often, they are for minor infractions, acts of survival, or simply being in the wrong place at the wrong time. A broken taillight, loitering, a minor marijuana possession – these seemingly trivial encounters become costly, life-altering events. Each citation, each arrest, carries with it a price tag. Fines, court fees, probation costs, the ever-present threat of a warrant for non-payment – these financial burdens quickly spiral out of control, transforming a moment of inconvenience into a crushing weight of debt. For families already living on the margins, this debt is not just an inconvenience; it is a slow, inexorable drain on resources that are already stretched thin. The money that should go towards rent, food, or education is instead siphoned off to pay for the privilege of having been caught in the system's machinery.

This financial bleed has a devastating ripple effect. A parent unable to pay a traffic ticket might face a license suspension, rendering them unable to commute to work. This leads to job loss, a loss that further exacerbates the family's financial precariousness. Children witness their parents' distress, the constant anxiety that permeates their home. Schools, already underfunded in these communities, suffer further as families are forced to relocate in search of cheaper housing, further destabilizing neighborhoods and disrupting educational continuity. The cycle of poverty, so often discussed in abstract terms, is given a brutal, material form by the financial penalties of the justice system. The revenue generated from these fines and fees, intended to fund public services, often perpetuates the very conditions that lead to further entanglement with the law. It's a perverse feedback loop, where the punishment for poverty becomes a mechanism for its perpetuation.

The consequences extend far beyond immediate financial hardship. The constant presence of law enforcement, the barrage of stops and searches, can create an atmosphere of perpetual surveillance and fear. Children grow up in environments where police officers are not seen as protectors, but as enforcers, agents of a system that seems designed to scrutinize and penalize them. This can lead to a deep-seated distrust of authority, a sense of alienation from the very institutions that are supposed to uphold justice. The psychological toll is immense. The stress of constant vigilance, the indignity of being routinely stopped and questioned, the fear of escalation – these experiences leave indelible marks, shaping individuals' perceptions of themselves and their place in society. This is not conducive to building resilient, thriving communities; it is the breeding ground for trauma and despair.

Moreover, the focus on punitive measures, driven by the demand for increased incarceration, often diverts resources and attention from programs that could genuinely address the root causes of crime. Instead of investing in education, job training, mental health services, and community development initiatives, vast sums are funneled into law enforcement and correctional facilities. This represents a profound misallocation of resources, a strategic choice that prioritizes punishment over prevention, warehousing individuals over rehabilitating them. The "tough on crime" rhetoric, so effectively deployed by lobbyists and special interests, masks a fundamental failure to invest in the human capital of these communities. When the primary response to social problems is to arrest and incarcerate, the underlying issues – poverty, lack of opportunity, inadequate education, and untreated mental illness – fester and grow, creating a self-perpetuating cycle of crime and punishment.

The concept of "community under siege" is not hyperbole; it is an accurate depiction of the lived experience in many of these areas. The aggressive enforcement of minor offenses, the imposition of crippling fines and fees, and the relentless pressure of surveillance create an environment where residents feel under constant threat. This siege mentality erodes social cohesion, fostering an atmosphere of suspicion and distrust. Neighbors become wary of each other, fearing that association with someone who has had a brush with the law could bring unwanted attention. The fabric of community life, already strained by economic hardship, is further frayed. The informal networks of support that are essential for community resilience are weakened when individuals are preoccupied with navigating the legal system and avoiding financial ruin.

The narrative of "justice" becomes twisted and distorted. For residents of these communities, the justice system often appears less about fairness and more about extraction. The courts become revenue-generating machines, and the police are seen as the collectors. The very idea of rehabilitation or restorative justice is pushed to the periphery, drowned out by the relentless demand for arrests, convictions, and the collection of fines. The laws, crafted and influenced by those who profit from incarceration, create a system where the presumption of innocence is often undermined by the practical realities of navigating a complex and punitive legal landscape. The path to redemption, or even just to a stable, law-abiding life, becomes an almost insurmountable obstacle course.

The impact on families is particularly heartbreaking. The incarceration of a parent, often the primary breadwinner, can plunge a family into immediate crisis. Children are left to navigate the world without a parent, often facing stigma and hardship. The emotional toll on both the incarcerated individual and their family is profound, leading to increased rates of depression, anxiety, and behavioral problems. The economic consequences are equally dire, with families losing income, facing increased expenses for communication and visitation, and often struggling to re-establish stability upon the individual's release. The system, rather than supporting families through difficult times, often serves to fracture them, exacerbating existing vulnerabilities and perpetuating cycles of disadvantage across generations.

This is the human cost, rendered in stark detail. It is the child who goes hungry because their parent's paycheck was garnished for court fees. It is the teenager who sees the school-to-prison pipeline as their most likely educational trajectory. It is the grandparent burdened with caring for grandchildren whose parents are behind bars. It is the pervasive sense of hopelessness that settles over communities where the promise of justice feels like a cruel joke, a system designed to extract wealth and perpetuate misery rather than to foster safety and well-being. The "unseen hand" of influence, far from being an abstract force, manifests as a tangible, suffocating pressure on the very foundations of community life, leaving behind a landscape of broken lives and shattered dreams. The impending doom is not a distant threat; it is the suffocating reality that grips these communities daily, a slow-motion catastrophe orchestrated from afar, and paid for with the lives and futures of those most vulnerable.

The suffocating grip of the carceral state, though designed to crush dissent and sow despair, had not entirely extinguished the human spirit. Beneath the veneer of enforced order, a subtle, yet potent, current of discontent began to flow, like subterranean water finding its way through bedrock. These were not the roaring protests that would later shake the foundations of established power, nor the meticulously organized legal challenges that would chip away at systemic injustice. Instead, these were whispers, tentative at first, but carrying the undeniable weight of shared experience and burgeoning awareness. They emerged from the very communities that had been most thoroughly dissected and commodified by the machinery of punishment, from the streets where the dragnet of fines and arrests tightened its noose with relentless efficiency.

It began with conversations exchanged over back fences, hushed tones in community centers, and late-night calls between concerned friends and family members. The sheer, unyielding pressure of the system, the constant drain on meager resources, the indignity of perpetual surveillance – these shared burdens were forging an unspoken solidarity. People who had once felt isolated in their struggles, believing their plight to be a personal failing, began to recognize a pattern. The seemingly random encounters with law enforcement, the insurmountable fines, the cascading consequences that stripped away jobs and dignity, were not isolated incidents. They were the product of a deliberate, if often opaque, system that seemed to have a vested interest in their marginalization.

In neighborhoods where the courthouse was a more familiar landmark than the library, where the siren song of the patrol car was a constant soundtrack, a new kind of awareness was dawning. It was a hard-won wisdom, etched into the faces of parents struggling to keep their children fed and housed while battling mounting legal debts. It was the grim understanding held by young men who saw the revolving door of juvenile detention as an almost preordained path. It was the quiet resilience of women who navigated the labyrinthine bureaucracy of probation and parole, their lives dictated by an endless series of appointments and payments, all to maintain even a sliver of autonomy.

These were the fertile grounds for the seeds of rebellion. They weren't sown by ideologues or agitators, but by ordinary people pushed to their breaking point. Consider the case of Maria, a single mother working two minimum-wage jobs to support her two children. A minor traffic infraction, a forgotten taillight, led to a citation that ballooned into a cascade of fines and fees. The inability to pay resulted in a suspended license, which in turn meant she could no longer reliably get to her second job. The threat of an arrest warrant loomed, a constant shadow over her already precarious existence. Maria's quiet desperation, her nights spent agonizing over how to make ends meet, was a microcosm of the suffering inflicted by the system. But her quiet desperation was evolving. She began speaking to her neighbors, sharing her story, and discovering that her experience was not unique. Their shared frustration, their collective weariness, began to coalesce into something more.

These conversations, initially characterized by resignation and anger, gradually began to shift towards a more active form of questioning. Why were certain neighborhoods policed with such aggressive fervor? Why did minor offenses carry such disproportionate financial penalties? Who benefited from this constant cycle of arrests and fines? These weren't abstract philosophical debates; they were urgent, practical inquiries born from the lived reality of systemic oppression. The whispers grew louder, morphing into a collective murmur of disbelief and defiance.

At the forefront of this nascent resistance were the grassroots organizations, often born out of necessity and sustained by the sheer will of their members. These were not well-funded think tanks or polished advocacy groups. They were often small, volunteer-run initiatives operating out of church basements, community center back rooms, or even someone's living room. They provided a crucial lifeline for those caught in the gears of the justice system. They offered help with navigating the complex maze of court procedures, assisted with applying for reduced fines, and provided support for individuals facing eviction or job loss due to legal entanglements.

One such organization, operating in a sprawling urban district choked by a dense network of courts and correctional facilities, called itself "The Bridge." Founded by a retired social worker named Eleanor Vance, The Bridge's mission was deceptively simple: to help people navigate the system and, more importantly, to challenge its fundamental unfairness. Eleanor, with her decades of experience witnessing the devastating impact of punitive policies, understood that true change would not come from legislative reform alone. It had to begin with empowering the people most affected.

The Bridge offered "Know Your Rights" workshops, where residents learned about their constitutional protections, how to interact with law enforcement, and the specific penalties associated with common citations in their area. These workshops, often attended by a mix of anxious teenagers, weary parents, and individuals recently released from incarceration, were more than just educational sessions. They were spaces where shared experiences could be voiced, where a sense of collective agency could begin to take root. Participants, initially hesitant and self-conscious, would gradually open up, their stories intertwining to paint a stark portrait of systemic injustice. The quiet nodding of heads, the shared sighs of recognition, were powerful affirmations that no one was alone in their struggle.

Beyond providing practical assistance, The Bridge also became a hub for nascent organizing. Small groups of residents, galvanized by their workshop experiences, began to meet independently, sharing strategies for dealing with police harassment or exploring ways to collectively petition local authorities to address issues like excessive fines. These were often individuals who had never engaged in activism before, their lives consumed by the daily struggle for survival. Yet, the sheer injustice they faced had ignited a spark of activism within them.

There was also the crucial work of families supporting incarcerated loved ones. The immense logistical and emotional toll of maintaining contact with a family member behind bars was staggering. The exorbitant costs of phone calls, the arduous visitation processes, the financial strain of supporting a family unit when a primary income earner was absent – these were the invisible burdens carried by countless families. In response, informal support networks began to emerge. Mothers, wives, and siblings would connect, sharing tips on navigating the prison system, pooling resources for phone cards, and offering each other emotional solace. These were acts of profound love and resilience, but they were also tinged with a growing awareness that the system was actively working to isolate and disempower them. Their quiet determination to maintain familial bonds in the face of such adversity was an implicit act of rebellion against a system that sought to fracture families.

One particularly poignant example of this grassroots spirit came from a small town in the Rust Belt, where a local factory closure had led to widespread unemployment and a dramatic increase in minor offenses, often driven by desperation. A group of mothers, whose children had been ensnared in the escalating juvenile justice system due to unpaid fines and probation violations, started meeting weekly. They called themselves "Mothers Against Unfair Fines." Their initial goal was simply to share information and support each other. But as they learned more about the punitive nature of the fines and fees, and the revenue-generating aspect of the local justice system, their objective began to broaden. They started writing letters to the local newspaper, sharing their stories and questioning the fairness of the system. They attended town hall meetings, their voices, though trembling, carrying a powerful moral weight as they spoke of the devastating impact of fines on their families.

These early acts of defiance, though seemingly small in scale, were crucial. They represented the first glimmers of a collective awakening, a refusal to accept the status quo. They were the planting of seeds in barren ground, the quiet murmurs that would, in time, grow into a chorus of dissent. The courage of these individuals, their willingness to speak out and organize in the face of overwhelming odds, was a testament to the enduring human capacity for resistance. They understood that silence, while perhaps offering a temporary shield, ultimately served the interests of those who profited from their oppression. By speaking, by connecting, by organizing, they were beginning to push back, to assert their humanity, and to sow the first fragile shoots of a movement that would eventually challenge the very foundations of the carceral state. The embers of discontent were glowing, waiting for the right conditions to ignite a larger fire.

Chapter 2: The Anatomy of Injustice

The scales of justice, depicted as a blindfolded figure, are a potent symbol, an aspiration so ingrained in the public consciousness that to question it feels akin to doubting gravity. We are taught from childhood that the courts are a sanctuary of impartiality, a place where truth, not prejudice, prevails, and where every individual stands before the law as an equal. This is the bedrock of our legal philosophy, the promise whispered in courtroom dramas and pledged in civic education. But scratch beneath the polished surface of this ideal, and one finds not an unblemished foundation, but a complex, often fraught, reality. The myth of blind justice is, in many respects, a carefully constructed facade, one that, when examined closely, reveals significant cracks, fissures that allow for the insidious intrusion of bias and influence, particularly when the stakes are high, and financial interests loom large.

The very human beings who don the black robes and preside over our courtrooms are not paragons of objective detachment. They are products of their environments, shaped by their upbringing, their education, their social circles, and their deeply held, often unarticulated, beliefs. These are not necessarily malicious intentions, but rather the subtle currents of implicit bias that can color perception and influence judgment. Think of the judge who, perhaps unconsciously, finds themselves more sympathetic to a defendant from a similar socioeconomic or racial background, or conversely, harbors a subconscious distrust of those perceived as "other." These biases, while not always overt, can manifest in countless subtle ways: in the tone of voice, the framing of questions, the interpretation of evidence, or even the length of a sentencing. The blindfold, intended to obscure external factors, can sometimes serve to conceal these internal lenses through which reality is filtered.

The political nature of judicial appointments further complicates the notion of impartiality. In many jurisdictions, judges are not chosen purely on merit but are either elected or appointed by political figures. This process inherently introduces a degree of subjectivity. Appointed judges, in particular, may owe their positions to the very politicians or parties that shaped the laws they are sworn to uphold. This can create a subtle, yet undeniable, pressure to conform to the prevailing political ideology or to rule in ways that are perceived as favorable to the appointing authority. While outright corruption is rare, the psychological weight of gratitude or the desire for reappointment can subtly steer a judge's decisions, especially in cases that touch upon politically sensitive issues or involve powerful interests. This is not about judges actively seeking to pervert justice, but about the systemic pressures that can nudge them, however imperceptibly, away from a truly neutral stance.

Consider the labyrinthine world of corporate litigation, where vast sums of money are on the table. In such arenas, the ideal of impartiality can be severely tested. Judges, like all individuals, are influenced by the information presented to them, and in complex financial cases, this information is often meticulously curated and presented by armies of highly paid lawyers. The sheer volume and technical complexity of financial data, expert testimony, and legal precedent can be overwhelming. In this environment, a judge might find themselves leaning on the arguments of counsel who present their case with greater clarity, conviction, or persuasive appeal, rather than necessarily the argument that is most legally sound. Furthermore, judges are often aware of the economic impact their rulings might have, not just on the parties involved, but on the broader business community, or even their own state's economy. This awareness, while stemming from a desire to serve the public good, can also introduce an external consideration that compromises the purely adversarial, truth-seeking process.

The pressure to conform to established norms and precedents also plays a significant role. The legal system, by its very nature, relies on consistency. Judges are trained to respect precedent, to build upon the decisions of those who came before them. While this is crucial for stability and predictability, it can also create a inertia that resists challenging established, and potentially flawed, legal interpretations. If a particular interpretation of a law has been consistently applied in a certain way, a judge might feel disinclined to deviate, even if they harbor private doubts about its fairness or efficacy. This adherence to established doctrine can become a form of institutional bias, a subtle endorsement of the status quo, even when that status quo demonstrably disadvantages certain groups or individuals.

The economic realities faced by the judiciary itself can also be a factor. While judges are generally well-compensated compared to the average citizen, their salaries are often set by legislative bodies. In times of fiscal austerity, or when facing pressure to keep taxes low, legislative bodies might be less inclined to approve significant pay raises for judges. This can create a subtle tension, a reliance on the goodwill of the legislative branch, which, in turn, can be influenced by the very corporate and special interests that frequently appear before the courts. The indirect economic pressures, the need for legislative approval for resources or future salary adjustments, can create an environment where a judge might be more hesitant to issue rulings that are perceived as overly adversarial to powerful economic forces.

Moreover, the psychological dynamics within a courtroom are intricate. A judge is in a position of immense authority. Lawyers are trained to persuade, and defendants, often overwhelmed and under-resourced, may struggle to effectively communicate their situation. The judge's perception of confidence, credibility, and even likeability can, consciously or unconsciously, influence their assessment of a case. A defendant who struggles to articulate their defense due to stress or lack of legal sophistication might be perceived as less credible than a well-spoken, articulate opponent, even if the underlying facts favor the former. This is where the blindfold becomes particularly problematic; it is meant to shield against external factors, but it cannot shield against the internal biases that shape how evidence and testimony are perceived.

The adversarial nature of the legal system, while designed to ensure all sides are heard, can also amplify biases. In cases involving significant financial stakes, the parties with the most resources can afford the most skilled legal teams, the most compelling expert witnesses, and the most extensive investigative resources. This creates an uneven playing field, and judges, tasked with impartially weighing the arguments presented, are often forced to make decisions based on the quality and quantity of the evidence and arguments put forth by each side. If one side can marshal vastly superior resources to construct a more persuasive narrative, even if that narrative deviates from the full truth, the judge may be compelled, by the rules of the system, to favor that narrative. The myth of blind justice falters when one litigant can essentially buy a more convincing reality than their opponent.

Consider cases involving intellectual property disputes or complex financial fraud. The defense of such cases requires immense financial backing, often provided by large corporations with significant legal departments. Small businesses or individual inventors, often the victims in these scenarios, simply cannot compete with the resources of their larger counterparts. They may present a valid claim, but without the ability to hire top-tier legal representation or to commission costly forensic accounting, their case may appear weaker in the eyes of the court. The judge, bound by the evidence presented, might find it difficult to overcome the sheer weight of resources deployed by the larger entity, leading to a decision that appears just on its face, but is fundamentally skewed by the economic disparity between the parties.

The concept of "judicial temperament" itself, often cited as a desirable quality in judges, can also be a double-edged sword. While an even-keeled demeanor is essential, it can also mask deeper biases. A judge who appears calm and dispassionate might, in fact, be operating under a set of deeply ingrained assumptions that they do not even recognize as biases. The ability to remain outwardly composed while inwardly harboring prejudice or favoring certain outcomes is a testament to the complexity of human psychology, and a significant challenge to the ideal of an impartial judiciary. The scales of justice are meant to be balanced by objective truth, but they can be subtly tilted by the subjective perceptions of the person holding them.

Furthermore, the pressure on judges to move cases through their dockets quickly can, paradoxically, undermine thoroughness and impartiality. Judicial efficiency is often measured by the number of cases processed. In a system where backlogs are common, judges may feel compelled to make decisions based on the information immediately available, rather than engaging in the exhaustive scrutiny that a truly just outcome might require. This is particularly concerning in areas where the consequences of a ruling are severe, such as in criminal sentencing or child custody disputes. The drive for efficiency can inadvertently favor expediency over meticulous justice, creating a system where speed, rather than fairness, becomes the primary metric of success.

The influence of legal scholarship and prevailing academic thought can also contribute to systemic biases. Judges often rely on established legal interpretations and scholarly commentary to inform their decisions. If a particular school of legal thought, which may itself be influenced by particular economic or social ideologies, becomes dominant, it can shape judicial thinking across the board. This creates a form of intellectual inertia, where judges are guided by a consensus that may not be entirely impartial or representative of the diverse needs of society. The blindfold, in this context, might be obscured by the glare of accepted wisdom.

The challenge, therefore, lies not in a clandestine conspiracy to pervert justice, but in the pervasive, often invisible, ways that human psychology, political realities, and economic pressures can subtly compromise the ideal of judicial impartiality. The myth of blind justice is a powerful aspiration, a necessary ideal to strive for. However, acknowledging the inherent vulnerabilities within the system is the first, crucial step towards mitigating their impact, ensuring that the scales, while perhaps not perfectly blind, are at least guided by a sincere and constant effort towards fairness and equity for all. It requires constant vigilance, a willingness to confront uncomfortable truths, and a commitment to reforming not just the laws, but the very processes through which justice is administered. The integrity of the system depends on our ability to see beyond the symbol of the blindfolded figure and to grapple with the complex human realities that shape judicial decision-making.

The edifice of American justice, so often held aloft as a beacon of fairness and due process, harbors a mechanism so potent it can bend the will of even the most resolute, so insidious it can manufacture guilt from the raw material of fear.

This mechanism is the plea bargain, a cornerstone of the modern criminal justice system, and a tool that, in the hands of an overstretched and outcome-driven prosecution, can morph into a formidable instrument of coercion. It is a Faustian bargain offered to defendants, a whispered temptation promising a swift escape from the potentially ruinous ordeal of a trial, but at a price that can shatter lives and erode the very notion of innocence until proven guilty. The chilling reality is that this system, designed to seek truth, frequently compels individuals to confess to crimes they did not commit, simply to mitigate the terrifying specter of a far more severe punishment.

Imagine the scene: a dimly lit interrogation room, the air thick with unspoken threats and the cold logic of the penal code. A defendant, perhaps young, perhaps bewildered by the labyrinthine legal process, sits across from a prosecutor. The charges are severe, the potential penalties draconian. The prosecutor, armed with the weight of the state and an intimate knowledge of sentencing guidelines, lays out the stark choice. "We can offer you X years," they might say, their voice a practiced blend of paternal concern and veiled menace, "if you plead guilty today. But if you insist on going to trial, and you lose – which you will, based on the evidence we have – you're looking at Y years, maybe even Z. And believe me, Y and Z are far, far worse than X." The numbers, X, Y, and Z, are not abstract concepts; they represent decades of a life extinguished behind bars, futures irrevocably lost.

This is not a negotiation between equals. It is a strategic maneuver, a calculated gamble where the prosecutor holds a stacked deck. The defendant, often without the financial resources for a robust defense, lacking the legal acumen to fully grasp the nuances of the evidence arrayed against them, and acutely aware of the jury's potential for bias, is placed in an untenable position. The fear of the unknown, amplified by the prosecutor's chilling predictions, becomes an overwhelming force. The presumption of innocence, a hallowed principle, begins to crumble under the sheer pressure of survival. The plea bargain, in this context, transforms from an opportunity for a mutually agreeable resolution into a weapon of coercion, designed to extract a guilty plea, regardless of actual culpability.

The "trial penalty" is a well-documented phenomenon. Studies have consistently shown that defendants who reject a plea offer and proceed to trial, even if acquitted, face significantly longer sentences if convicted than they would have if they had accepted the initial plea. This disparity creates a powerful disincentive to exercise the fundamental right to a trial. Why risk a potential lifetime behind bars for the slim chance of an acquittal, especially when the system itself seems to telegraph a foregone conclusion? The prosecutor's confident assertion of guilt, the perceived strength of their evidence (often presented without the full counter-arguments that a trial would allow), and the stark contrast between the offered sentence and the potential maximum sentence all conspire to push the defendant towards accepting the deal.

Consider the case of individuals who are genuinely innocent. They may have been in the wrong place at the wrong time, wrongly identified, or caught in a web of circumstantial evidence. They maintain their innocence, but the specter of a life-altering sentence looms large. Their lawyer, though perhaps fighting valiantly, may be unable to entirely assuage their client's fear. The prosecutor, privy to the defendant's desperation, can leverage this fear with ruthless efficiency. The offer of X years, while still a substantial punishment, suddenly appears as a lifeline, a way to preserve some semblance of freedom, to see loved ones again, to avoid the complete annihilation of their existence. In such moments, the truth of their innocence can become a secondary concern, overshadowed by the primal urge for self-preservation.

This is where the "coerced confession" aspect of plea bargaining becomes particularly alarming. While not a confession extracted through physical torture, it is a confession born of extreme psychological duress. The defendant isn't admitting guilt because they are guilty; they are admitting guilt because the legal system, through the mechanism of plea bargaining and the threat of the trial penalty, has made it the most rational, albeit tragic, choice for survival. The system, in its relentless pursuit of efficiency and conviction rates, effectively incentivizes the innocent to plead guilty. This is a profound perversion of justice, a scenario where the very act of seeking redress through a trial becomes a punitive measure in itself.

The statistics are staggering. The vast majority of criminal cases in the United States – upwards of 95% – are resolved through plea bargains, not trials. This overwhelming reliance on plea deals has fundamentally reshaped the nature of criminal adjudication. It has created a system where the "trial" has become an anomaly, a rare event reserved for the most extreme or strategically advantageous cases. For the average defendant, the path to resolution is predetermined: a negotiation with the prosecution, a calculated risk assessment, and ultimately, a plea. This reality can lead to a chilling effect, where potential defenses are never fully explored, where wrongful convictions are solidified, and where the pursuit of justice takes a backseat to the efficient processing of cases.

The prosecutor, in this scenario, wields immense power. They control the charging decisions, the evidence presented (or withheld), and the offers made. They can, intentionally or unintentionally, overcharge defendants to create more leverage for plea negotiations. They can present a seemingly overwhelming case, even if key pieces of evidence are weak or potentially exculpatory, knowing that the defendant is unlikely to risk a trial to challenge them. This power imbalance is a critical flaw. While many prosecutors are dedicated public servants striving for justice, the systemic pressures within the criminal justice system can incentivize a different kind of behavior: securing convictions, managing caseloads, and maintaining high win rates. A plea bargain, regardless of the defendant's actual guilt, achieves all of these objectives.

The consequences for individuals who accept plea bargains under duress are devastating. They carry the mark of a conviction, often for life. This can lead to the loss of employment opportunities, housing, the right to vote, and the ability to maintain family relationships. They may be stigmatized as criminals, even if they never committed the offense they admitted to. Their reputation, their future, and their very sense of self can be irrevocably damaged. And all of this can stem from a decision made not out of guilt, but out of sheer terror and a desperate attempt to escape a system that offers little in the way of genuine recourse when faced with overwhelming odds.

Furthermore, the efficiency argument, while often cited as a justification for plea bargaining, masks a deeper problem. By encouraging defendants to plead guilty, the system avoids the time, expense, and uncertainty of trials. This allows courts to process a higher volume of cases. However, this efficiency comes at a profound cost: the erosion of fundamental rights and the potential for widespread injustice. It prioritizes throughput over thoroughness, conviction rates over the meticulous pursuit of truth. It creates a system where the appearance of justice – the swift processing of cases and the high number of convictions – can overshadow the reality of justice, which demands that the innocent be protected and that guilt be proven beyond a reasonable doubt, not merely negotiated.

The pressure to plea bargain can be exacerbated by factors such as race, socioeconomic status, and access to legal representation. Defendants from marginalized communities, often with limited financial means and facing systemic biases within the justice system, may be even more vulnerable to prosecutorial pressure. They may be less likely to trust the system, more intimidated by the process, and more desperate for a resolution that offers a semblance of control over their chaotic circumstances. In such cases, the plea bargain can become a tool that disproportionately impacts already vulnerable populations, reinforcing existing inequalities and perpetuating cycles of injustice.

The narrative of the "guilty" defendant who intelligently chooses a plea bargain to mitigate their sentence is a common one, and often true. But it is only one facet of a much larger, more disturbing picture. The reality is that for a significant number of individuals, the plea bargain is not a choice, but a surrender. It is a capitulation to a system that has effectively weaponized fear and uncertainty against them. It is a mechanism that, by its very design, can pressure the innocent to confess, thereby short-circuiting the pursuit of truth and cementing convictions that may be based on nothing more than a strategic decision for self-preservation. This "prosecutor's ploy" is not merely a procedural shortcut; it is a fundamental challenge to the integrity of the American justice system, a silent but devastating force that can render the promise of due process a hollow echo for too many. The blindfold of justice can indeed be manipulated, and in the realm of plea bargaining, the scales are too often tipped not by evidence, but by the chilling weight of fear.

The clang of the cell door doesn't just signify confinement; for the wrongly convicted, it echoes with a profound, soul-crushing betrayal. It's the sound of a life irrevocably derailed, not by their own transgressions, but by the gaping fissures in the very system designed to uphold justice. The edifice of the American justice system, so meticulously constructed on the bedrock of due process and the presumption of innocence, harbors within it a dark undercurrent where the innocent can become, and remain, its most tragic casualties. These are not mere statistical anomalies; they are flesh-and-blood individuals, stripped of their liberty, their reputations, and their futures, locked away for crimes they did not commit. The mechanism of wrongful conviction is a multifaceted tragedy, a perfect storm of human error, systemic blind spots, and at times, outright malfeasance, all conspiring to enscrew an innocent soul within the iron jaws of incarceration.

The genesis of these miscarriages of justice is as varied as it is disturbing. Consider the chilling specter of flawed forensic science. Once held as the unassailable arbiters of truth, forensic disciplines have been revealed to harbor inherent uncertainties and, in some cases, outright fallibility. Hair and fiber analysis, bite mark comparisons, even eyewitness testimony, once considered highly reliable, have been subjected to rigorous re-examination, revealing significant limitations and susceptibility to subjective interpretation. The advent of DNA technology, a true game-changer in the pursuit of justice, has not only exonerated the innocent but has also served as a stark indictment of past investigative and judicial practices. It has illuminated instances where contaminated samples, improper analysis, or even outright fabrication of results have led to the conviction of innocent individuals. Imagine a scenario where a microscopic fiber, indistinguishable to the naked eye, becomes the linchpin of a prosecution, leading a jury to believe it places the defendant at a crime scene, when in reality, its presence is coincidental or, worse, a product of a flawed testing protocol. The weight of such "scientific" evidence, presented by seemingly authoritative experts, can be almost impossible for a layperson, or even a seasoned defense attorney without specialized knowledge, to counter. The assumption of scientific infallibility, often implicitly or explicitly communicated to juries, creates a dangerous presumption of guilt that can be incredibly difficult to dismantle.

Beyond the realm of scientific fallibility lies the more sinister dimension of prosecutorial misconduct. While the vast majority of prosecutors are dedicated public servants, the immense power vested in their office, coupled with the immense pressure to secure convictions, can, in rare but devastating instances, lead to abuses. This can manifest in a multitude of ways. The deliberate withholding of exculpatory evidence – evidence that points towards the defendant's innocence – is a cardinal sin in the legal world, a direct violation of

Brady v. Maryland. Yet, such violations have occurred, leaving defendants to face charges without the benefit of crucial information that could have cleared their names. This isn't always a grand conspiracy; it can be a subtle omission, a piece of evidence deemed insignificant by a busy prosecutor that later proves to be the key to unlocking an innocent person's freedom.

Another insidious tactic is the use of unreliable informants or witnesses, whose testimony might be coerced, incentivized through reduced sentences or financial reward, or based on demonstrable falsehoods. Prosecutors may exploit the desperation of incarcerated individuals, offering leniency in exchange for testimony against another defendant, regardless of the truthfulness of that testimony. This creates a perverse incentive structure where the pursuit of justice is supplanted by the pursuit of convictions, even if those convictions are built on a foundation of sand. The spectacle of a star witness, whose credibility is later exposed as dubious, recanting their testimony after an innocent person has spent years, even decades, behind bars, is a recurring nightmare in the wrongful conviction narrative. The sheer audacity of such deception, and the system's initial failure to detect it, gnaws at the very core of our belief in justice.

Then there is the stark reality of inadequate defense counsel. The Sixth Amendment guarantees the right to counsel, but the quality of that representation can vary wildly, particularly for indigent defendants who rely on overburdened public defender systems. Lawyers tasked with managing caseloads that would overwhelm a small army can struggle to dedicate the time and resources necessary for a thorough investigation, expert consultation, or the meticulous crafting of a defense. In such circumstances, even the most well-intentioned attorney may be unable to effectively challenge the prosecution's case, leaving their client vulnerable to wrongful conviction. Imagine a scenario where a crucial alibi witness is never contacted because the defense attorney simply doesn't have the time to track them down, or where critical forensic evidence is not challenged because the defense cannot afford an independent expert. These are not hypothetical dangers; they are the grim realities that plague countless defendants, pushing them towards plea bargains or, worse, trials where their defense is a mere shadow of what it could have been.

The sheer difficulty of overturning a wrongful conviction, once it has taken root, is a testament to the system's inherent inertia and, at times, its protective instincts. The legal avenues for challenging a conviction are complex and fraught with procedural hurdles. Habeas corpus petitions, the primary mechanism for challenging unlawful detention, are notoriously difficult to win. Courts are often hesitant to revisit decisions, particularly when they involve a lengthy passage of time, as memories fade, evidence degrades, and the initial verdict is presumed to be correct. The presumption of finality, while necessary for the efficient functioning of the legal system, can become an insurmountable barrier for the innocent seeking to prove their innocence.

The "conviction integrity unit" or similar post-conviction review mechanisms, established in some jurisdictions to address wrongful convictions, are a hopeful development, but they are not a panacea. Their effectiveness can be hampered by limited resources, political will, and the inherent challenge of re-examining cases that have long since been closed. The burden of proof often remains overwhelmingly on the convicted individual, who must not only demonstrate their innocence but also overcome the legal presumptions that uphold their original conviction. This can feel like an Sisyphean task, pushing a boulder uphill against the relentless force of established legal precedent and bureaucratic resistance.

The psychological toll on those who have been wrongly convicted is profound and often irreparable. Years, or even decades, spent in the dehumanizing environment of prison, the constant gnawing fear, the loss of personal relationships, the erosion of self-worth – these are wounds that do not easily heal, even after release. The reentry into society can be a bewildering and isolating experience. The world has moved on, and the individual, carrying the indelible stigma of a criminal record, faces immense challenges in finding employment, housing, and regaining a sense of normalcy. The trust in institutions, particularly the justice system, is shattered, often replaced by a deep-seated cynicism and a sense of permanent alienation. They are no longer simply "former inmates"; they are survivors of a profound injustice, forever marked by their experience.

The narrative of wrongful conviction is not merely a collection of isolated incidents; it is a systemic indictment. It speaks to the fallibility of human judgment, the limitations of our investigative and forensic tools, and the inherent biases that can permeate any human institution. It highlights the critical need for continuous reform, for rigorous oversight, and for a willingness to confront uncomfortable truths about the imperfections within our justice system. The innocent who are imprisoned are not simply victims of bad luck; they are a stark reminder that the pursuit of justice is an ongoing, imperfect, and at times, perilous journey, one that demands constant vigilance and an unwavering commitment to ensuring that the scales of justice are not merely balanced, but are impeccably true. The system's blind eye, though sometimes born of oversight or overwork, can inflict a lifetime of damage.

The courtroom doors, often grand and imposing, are merely the antechamber to a far more formidable structure: the prison. For the accused, the journey from the hushed solemnity of a judge's chambers to the stark, echoing corridors of a correctional facility is a descent. It's a process relentlessly efficient in its conveyance, yet often devastatingly indifferent to the individual humanity it processes. This is the prison pipeline, a conduit through which lives are irrevocably channeled, often guided by forces beyond the individual's control, and disproportionately impacting those already navigating the precarious edges of society. The gears of this machine grind with a formidable momentum, driven by a complex interplay of legal statutes, judicial discretion, and socio-economic realities.

At the heart of this relentless flow lies the sentencing phase. Here, the abstract pronouncements of law collide with the lived experiences of defendants, and the disparities can be stark, even brutal. Mandatory minimum sentences, a legislative tool intended to ensure a baseline level of punishment, have proven to be a particularly potent force in widening the prison pipeline. These laws strip judges of crucial discretion, forcing them to impose predetermined lengths of incarceration, regardless of the nuances of a case or the individual circumstances of the offender. A minor role in a drug conspiracy, for instance, can trigger the same draconian sentence as that meted out to a kingpin, simply because the quantity of drugs involved crossed an arbitrary legislative threshold. This rigid application of the law can transform what might have been a rehabilitative opportunity into a life-altering sentence, effectively warehousing individuals for extended periods, often with little regard for their potential for change or their minimal culpability. The human cost of such inflexibility is immeasurable, as lives are frozen in time, families are fractured, and communities are destabilized.

This rigidity is often compounded by the sheer volume of cases that inundate the court system. The efficiency demanded by overloaded dockets can inadvertently favor outcomes that expedite processing over those that ensure thorough individual justice. Plea bargains, while a necessary tool for managing caseloads, can become a coercive instrument. Faced with the prospect of lengthy mandatory sentences if convicted at trial, and often represented by overworked public defenders with insufficient resources, defendants may feel compelled to accept plea deals, even if they maintain their innocence. The implicit threat of a significantly harsher sentence hangs heavy in the air, a silent accomplice to the prosecutor's offer. This can lead to individuals pleading guilty to crimes they did not commit, simply to escape the even greater peril of a trial and the potential for a devastatingly severe sentence under mandatory minimum regimes. The pressure to "do the time" for a crime they didn't commit, rather than risk doing even more time for a conviction they might not have deserved, is a grim calculus that plays out in courtrooms across the nation daily.

The demographics of this pipeline are not accidental. Decades of research and lived experience have laid bare the undeniable truth: the prison pipeline disproportionately funnels individuals from marginalized communities into the carceral system. Racial and ethnic minorities, particularly Black and Hispanic populations, are incarcerated at rates significantly higher than their white counterparts, even when accounting for similar rates of offending. This disparity is not a reflection of inherent criminality, but rather a complex tapestry woven from threads of systemic racism, socio-economic disadvantage, and biased policing practices. Communities subjected to aggressive, over-policing are more likely to have their residents arrested, charged, and processed through the courts. Poverty, lack of educational opportunities, and limited access to resources further exacerbate vulnerability, creating a cycle where individuals are more likely to come into contact with the justice system and less likely to have the means to mount an effective defense. The intersection of race and poverty acts as a powerful accelerant, pushing already disadvantaged individuals further into the maw of the justice system.

Once processed through the courtroom and subjected to sentencing, the individual enters the physical reality of incarceration. This is not merely a period of deprivation of liberty; it is an experience designed, in many ways, to strip away identity and foster conformity. Overcrowding is a pervasive problem in many correctional facilities, a direct consequence of the sheer volume of individuals being processed through the pipeline. Cell blocks designed for a certain capacity are often packed far beyond their intended limits. This intense proximity breeds tension, exacerbates existing health issues, and strains already limited resources. The constant hum of humanity, confined and stressed, creates an environment that is inherently volatile and psychologically taxing. Sleep is interrupted, personal space is non-existent, and the basic dignity of privacy is a luxury few can afford.

The underfunding of correctional facilities further exacerbates these conditions. Insufficient budgets translate into understaffed institutions, leading to longer wait times for basic services, less time for meaningful programming, and a diminished capacity for effective oversight. Security personnel are stretched thin, often leading to a reliance on reactive measures rather than proactive interventions. Educational and vocational programs, critical for rehabilitation and successful reentry, are often the first casualties of budget cuts. The lack of meaningful opportunities for self-improvement can leave individuals feeling hopeless and resigned, reinforcing the cycle of recidivism rather than breaking it. The pursuit of a meaningful existence is replaced by a daily struggle for survival within the confines of the institution.

The physical environment itself can be a source of chronic stress and dehumanization. Dilapidated facilities, inadequate sanitation, and a lack of access to quality healthcare contribute to a pervasive sense of neglect. Chronic illnesses can go untreated, mental health crises can be mishandled, and the general wear and tear on the body and mind is significant. The food served is often of poor quality and insufficient quantity, contributing to malnutrition and further degrading the sense of care. These are not luxuries; these are the basic necessities that contribute to an individual's well-being and their capacity to maintain a semblance of health and dignity. When these are systematically denied, the experience of incarceration becomes a profound assault on the human spirit.

Moreover, the very architecture of the prison is designed to reinforce a sense of powerlessness and control. The constant surveillance, the rigid schedules, the arbitrary enforcement of rules – all contribute to an environment where individual agency is severely curtailed. The clang of gates, the shouted commands, the pervasive sense of being watched – these sensory inputs become the soundtrack to a life lived under constant duress. The loss of autonomy extends to the most basic aspects of life: what to wear, when to eat, when to sleep, whom to associate with. This relentless control, while ostensibly for security, can have a devastating impact on an individual's sense of self and their ability to make independent decisions.

The concept of "justice" within this context takes on a chillingly utilitarian hue. The economic realities of a society that increasingly relies on incarceration as a solution to social problems cannot be ignored. The privatization of prisons, for instance, introduces profit motives into the equation, creating an incentive to maintain high occupancy rates. This can influence legislative decisions, lobbying efforts, and the overall approach to criminal justice, shifting the focus from rehabilitation and crime prevention to the mere warehousing of individuals. The construction and maintenance of prisons, the provision of services within them, all represent significant economic interests, creating a vested stake in the continued expansion of the carceral system.

The dehumanizing aspects of incarceration are not merely incidental; they are, in many ways, intrinsic to the system's functioning. Labeling individuals as "inmates" or "offenders" rather than as people with histories, families, and potential futures reinforces their status as objects to be managed. The reduction of individuals to a number, a file, a set of behaviors to be controlled, erodes their individuality and makes it easier for the system to operate with a degree of detachment. This detachment, while perhaps necessary for the staff to perform their duties, contributes to the perpetuation of inhumane conditions.

The true cost of "justice" as meted out through this pipeline is therefore not solely measured in dollars and cents, or even in the sheer number of individuals behind bars. It is measured in the fractured families, the lost potential, the intergenerational cycles of poverty and incarceration, and the erosion of trust in institutions. It is measured in the psychological scars left on individuals, many of whom will carry the weight of their experiences long after their release, facing insurmountable barriers to reintegration. The prison pipeline, from its inception in the courtroom to its grim conclusion in the cellblock, represents a systemic failure to uphold the principles of justice, disproportionately impacting the most vulnerable and perpetuating a cycle of harm that extends far beyond the confines of any correctional facility. It is a stark testament to how a system designed to dispense justice can, in practice, become an engine of profound injustice, fueled by rigid laws, overwhelming caseloads, and deeply entrenched societal inequalities.

The bars of a courtroom, however imposing, are merely a prelude to the starker reality that awaits. Beyond the hushed pronouncements and the sterile formality of legal proceedings lies the true engine of transformation, or rather, deconstruction: the prison. For those ensnared by the justice system, the transition from the relative normalcy of civilian life to the regimented, often brutal, existence within correctional facilities is not merely a change of address; it is an abrupt, often violent, severance from the world they knew. This is the prison pipeline, a conduit through which lives are not just channeled, but often irrevocably rerouted, propelled by forces frequently beyond individual control, and with a devastating predilection for those already teetering on the precipice of society. The gears of this formidable machine, driven by a complex interplay of statutory mandates, judicial discretion, and the harsh realities of socio-economic disparity, grind with an unyielding momentum.

At the very heart of this relentless flow lies the sentencing phase, where the abstract pronouncements of law clash violently with the lived, and often desperate, realities of defendants. Here, the disparities can be not just noticeable, but stark, even brutal. Mandatory minimum sentences, legislated with the purported aim of ensuring a baseline of punitive consistency, have emerged as a particularly potent force in widening the prison pipeline. These laws, with their inflexible mandates, effectively strip judges of their crucial discretionary powers, compelling them to impose predetermined lengths of incarceration. This applies irrespective of the unique nuances of a specific case or the deeply personal circumstances of the offender. Consider, for example, a low-level participant in a drug conspiracy, a mere courier perhaps, whose direct culpability might be minimal. Yet, because the quantity of narcotics involved transgressed an arbitrary legislative threshold, they can find themselves facing the same draconian sentence as a hardened kingpin orchestrating the entire operation. This rigid application of legal tenets can transform what might have been a valuable opportunity for rehabilitation into a life-altering sentence, effectively warehousing individuals for extended periods, often with a callous disregard for their potential for change or their limited degree of culpability. The human cost of such inflexibility is truly immeasurable, as lives are effectively frozen in time, families are systematically fractured, and communities are destabilized.

This pervasive rigidity is frequently compounded by the sheer, overwhelming volume of cases that inundate the court system. The relentless pressure for efficiency, a necessary evil born from overloaded dockets, can inadvertently favor outcomes that expedite processing over those that painstakingly ensure individual justice. Plea bargains, while undoubtedly a vital tool for managing the sheer weight of caseloads, can too easily morph into a coercive instrument. Faced with the chilling prospect of lengthy mandatory sentences should they be convicted at trial—a prospect made all the more terrifying by often overworked public defenders who lack the time and resources to mount a robust defense—defendants can feel an overwhelming compulsion to accept plea deals. This is true even if they steadfastly maintain their innocence. The implicit, ever-present threat of a significantly harsher sentence hangs heavy in the air, a silent, insidious accomplice to the prosecutor's seemingly magnanimous offer. This coercive dynamic can, and often does, lead to individuals pleading guilty to crimes they did not commit, simply to escape the even greater peril of a trial and the potential for a devastatingly severe sentence dictated by mandatory minimum regimes. The grim calculus, the agonizing decision to "do the time" for a crime one did not perpetrate, rather than risk doing even more time for a conviction one might not have deserved, is a stark reality that plays out in courtrooms across the nation on a daily basis.

The demographic contours of this pipeline are not a matter of chance or happenstance. Decades of rigorous research and the raw, often painful, testimony of lived experience have unequivocally laid bare a truth that can no longer be ignored: the prison pipeline disproportionately funnels individuals from marginalized communities into the carceral system. Racial and ethnic minorities, particularly Black and Hispanic populations, are incarcerated at rates that are alarmingly and disproportionately higher than their white counterparts, even when rigorous statistical analyses account for similar rates of offending. This stark disparity is not, and never has been, a reflection of any inherent criminality within these groups. Rather, it is the product of a complex, interwoven tapestry woven from the threads of systemic racism, profound socio-economic disadvantage, and the deeply embedded biases within policing practices. Communities that are subjected to aggressive, over-policing are inherently more likely to have their residents arrested, charged, and subsequently processed through the courts. Poverty, a dire lack of educational opportunities, and severely limited access to essential resources further exacerbate vulnerability, creating a vicious cycle where individuals are not only more likely to come into contact with the justice system but also far less likely to possess the financial or social capital necessary to mount an effective defense. The relentless intersection of race and poverty acts as a powerful accelerant, relentlessly pushing already disadvantaged individuals further into the insatiable maw of the justice system.

Once an individual has been processed through the labyrinthine corridors of the courtroom and subjected to the finality of a sentencing decree, they enter the stark, unforgiving physical reality of incarceration. This is not merely a period of enforced deprivation of liberty; it is an experience meticulously designed, in many respects, to strip away individual identity and to forcefully foster an atmosphere of unyielding conformity. Overcrowding stands as a pervasive and deeply troubling problem within a vast majority of correctional facilities, a direct and predictable consequence of the sheer, unmanageable volume of individuals being processed relentlessly through the pipeline. Cell blocks, originally designed and engineered to accommodate a specific capacity, are frequently packed far beyond their intended limits, creating an environment of intense human proximity. This proximity, in turn, breeds palpable tension, exacerbates existing and often chronic health issues, and strains already woefully limited resources to their breaking point. The constant, unsettling hum of humanity, confined and perpetually stressed, creates an atmosphere that is inherently volatile, unpredictable, and psychologically taxing to an extreme degree. Sleep is constantly interrupted, personal space is a non-existent luxury, and the fundamental human dignity of privacy becomes an unattainable aspiration for the vast majority.

The chronic underfunding of correctional facilities further intensifies and exacerbates these already dire conditions. Insufficient budgetary allocations inevitably translate into understaffed institutions, leading to interminable wait times for even the most basic services, severely curtailed opportunities for meaningful rehabilitative programming, and a diminished capacity for effective oversight and intervention. Security personnel, stretched impossibly thin, are often forced into a reactive stance rather than being able to implement proactive, preventative measures. Educational and vocational programs, which are absolutely critical for genuine rehabilitation and the successful reintegration of individuals back into society, are frequently the first casualties of stringent budget cuts. The stark absence of meaningful opportunities for self-improvement can leave individuals feeling utterly hopeless and resigned to their fate, thereby reinforcing the debilitating cycle of recidivism rather than offering any real hope of breaking it. The innate human pursuit of a meaningful existence is brutally replaced by a daily, grinding struggle for mere survival within the oppressive confines of the institution.

The physical environment itself—the decaying infrastructure, the inadequate sanitation, the severe lack of access to quality healthcare—becomes a constant source of chronic stress and profound dehumanization. Chronic illnesses can go untreated for extended periods, mental health crises can be tragically mishandled or ignored entirely, and the general wear and tear on both the body and the mind is simply immense. The food provided within these facilities is often of exceptionally poor quality and insufficient quantity, contributing significantly to malnutrition and further degrading any semblance of care or consideration. These are not perceived as luxuries; they are the fundamental necessities that contribute immeasurably to an individual's overall well-being and their intrinsic capacity to maintain a basic state of health and dignity. When these essential elements are systematically denied, the experience of incarceration transcends mere punishment and becomes a profound, soul-crushing assault on the very human spirit.

Furthermore, the very architectural design and operational ethos of the prison are meticulously engineered to reinforce a pervasive sense of powerlessness and absolute control. The unblinking, constant surveillance, the rigidly enforced schedules that dictate every moment of the day, the often arbitrary and capricious enforcement of rules—all contribute to creating an environment where individual agency is severely curtailed, if not entirely eliminated. The incessant clang of gates, the amplified, often aggressive, shouted commands, the pervasive, suffocating sense of being perpetually watched—these sensory inputs become the grim, unyielding soundtrack to a life lived under constant, debilitating duress. The loss of autonomy extends to the most basic, fundamental aspects of daily life: what one wears, when one eats, when one is permitted to sleep, whom one is allowed to associate with. This relentless, all-encompassing control, while ostensibly justified in the name of security, can have a devastating and long-lasting impact on an individual's sense of self-worth and their fundamental ability to make independent, rational decisions.

Within this grim context, the very concept of "justice" begins to acquire a chillingly utilitarian and perversely economic hue. The undeniable economic realities of a society that has increasingly come to rely on incarceration as a primary solution to a wide array of social problems cannot and must not be ignored. The privatization of prisons, for instance, introduces potent profit motives directly into the equation, thereby creating a powerful incentive to maintain high occupancy rates. This financial imperative can, and often does, exert significant influence on legislative decisions, fuels aggressive lobbying efforts, and fundamentally shapes the overall approach to criminal justice, shifting the primary focus away from rehabilitation and genuine crime prevention towards the mere, passive warehousing of individuals. The construction and ongoing maintenance of prisons, the provision of goods and services within their walls, all represent significant economic interests, thereby creating a vested, material stake in the continued, and often exponential, expansion of the carceral system.

The dehumanizing aspects of incarceration are not merely incidental footnotes; they are, in many profound ways, intrinsic to the very functioning and perpetuation of the system itself. The deliberate labeling of individuals as mere "inmates" or "offenders," rather than as complex human beings with rich histories, cherished families, and boundless future potential, effectively reinforces their status as mere objects to be managed and controlled. The reduction of individuals to a number, a case file, a set of behaviors to be meticulously controlled, inexorably erodes their individuality and makes it considerably easier for the system to operate with a degree of cold, impersonal detachment. This detachment, while perhaps a psychological coping mechanism necessary for the staff to perform their demanding duties, ultimately contributes significantly to the perpetuation of inhumane conditions.

The true, overarching cost of "justice" as it is so often dispensed through this relentless pipeline is therefore not solely measured in abstract dollars and cents, or even in the stark, quantifiable number of individuals confined behind bars. It is measured in the devastatingly fractured families, the tragically lost potential of millions, the intergenerational cycles of poverty and incarceration that ensnare entire communities, and the profound erosion of trust in the very institutions that are meant to uphold fairness and equality. It is measured in the deep, psychological scars that are left on individuals, many of whom will carry the indelible weight of their experiences long after their official release, facing insurmountable barriers to successful reintegration into society. The prison pipeline, from its very inception in the sterile, often impersonal courtroom to its grim, suffocating conclusion in the echoing cellblock, represents a catastrophic systemic failure to uphold the fundamental principles of justice. It disproportionately impacts the most vulnerable members of society and relentlessly perpetuates a cycle of harm and despair that extends far beyond the physical confines of any correctional facility. It stands as a stark, undeniable testament to how a system ostensibly designed to dispense justice can, in its practical application, become a powerful engine of profound, systemic injustice, fueled by rigidly inflexible laws, overwhelming caseloads, and deeply entrenched, pervasive societal inequalities.

The echoes of injustice reverberate far beyond the concrete walls of prisons and the hushed halls of courthouses. They permeate the very fabric of families and communities, leaving behind a wake of devastation that can span generations. When an individual is removed from their home and confined, especially when that individual is a parent, a spouse, or a primary breadwinner, the consequences are immediate and often catastrophic. The economic stability of a household can crumble in an instant. Bills go unpaid, mortgages default, and children are left to navigate a world stripped of a crucial source of support and guidance. This economic hardship is not a temporary inconvenience; it often becomes a permanent scar, pushing families deeper into poverty and making the prospect of a stable future feel like an impossible dream. The burden falls disproportionately on women and children, who are left to shoulder the emotional and financial weight of their loved one's absence, often with limited resources and facing societal stigma.

The emotional toll is equally, if not more, devastating. Children of incarcerated parents often experience higher rates of anxiety, depression, and behavioral problems. They grapple with the shame and secrecy surrounding their parent's incarceration, facing the difficult task of explaining absences and hardships to peers and teachers. The trauma of separation, the uncertainty of return, and the often-harsh realities of prison visits create deep emotional wounds that can take a lifetime to heal. This emotional scarring can manifest in a variety of ways, impacting their ability to form healthy relationships, their academic performance, and their overall mental well-being. The absence of a parent figure can also lead to a lack of positive role modeling, leaving young people more vulnerable to negative influences and potentially perpetuating a cycle of crime and incarceration. The phrase "generations of incarceration" is not hyperbole; it is a lived reality for countless families who see their children follow the same tragic path as their parents, caught in a seemingly inescapable loop.

Communities, too, bear the brunt of mass incarceration. The removal of a significant portion of their population, often concentrated in specific neighborhoods, erodes social capital and weakens community bonds. When productive members of a community are incarcerated, essential skills, leadership, and social networks are lost. This can lead to increased crime rates, reduced economic activity, and a general decline in community well-being. The physical landscape of some neighborhoods can even reflect this phenomenon, with an increase in vacant homes and a visible absence of young men. The social infrastructure that supports a thriving community—local businesses, community organizations, and informal support systems—is weakened when its members are systematically removed. This creates a vicious cycle where disadvantaged communities, already struggling with poverty and lack of opportunity, are further destabilized by the punitive reach of the justice system.

The "tyranny tax," a term that captures the multifaceted burdens imposed by mass incarceration, extends far beyond the monetary fines, fees, and surcharges that are often levied against individuals and their families. It is a tax on human potential, a tax on familial bonds, and a tax on the very soul of communities. The economic costs are astronomical, not just in terms of the direct expenses of building and maintaining prisons, but also in the lost productivity, the foregone tax revenue, and the increased demand for social services for families struggling in the wake of incarceration. However, the immeasurable human cost, the stories of shattered dreams, broken families, and lost opportunities, is what truly defines the devastating ripple effect of the American justice system. It is a cost that cannot be fully quantified, yet its impact is felt in every corner of society, a constant reminder of the profound injustices that lie at the heart of the system. This pervasive, insidious influence transforms individual tragedies into systemic failures, leaving an indelible mark on millions of lives and communities across the nation. The damage inflicted is not confined to the time served behind bars; it is a lingering wound that festers, impacting generations and undermining the very notion of a just and equitable society.

Chapter 3: The Absence of Empathy

The siren's wail, once a sound of desperate urgency, has morphed into a percussive punctuation mark in the symphony of American streets. It's a sound that now often signals not just the arrival of help, but the imminent application of overwhelming force. This isn't the same force that once sought to merely maintain order; this is a force honed, equipped, and trained with the explicit purpose of overwhelming an adversary. We are witnessing the insidious creep of militarization into domestic law enforcement, a transformation that is fundamentally altering the relationship between those sworn to protect and the communities they serve. The former officer, a figure once envisioned as a community guardian, a relatable presence, is increasingly becoming an enforcer, a soldier in a domestic war that has no clear front lines, only blurred boundaries and escalating casualties.

The visual cues are stark and unavoidable. Patrol cars, once utilitarian vehicles designed for transport and visibility, have been replaced by armored personnel carriers, their hulking frames and reinforced exteriors broadcasting an unmistakable message: this is not a neighborhood, it's a battlefield. SWAT teams, initially conceived as specialized units for high-risk hostage situations and tactical operations, are now routinely deployed for routine arrests, their tactical gear and overwhelming firepower becoming the default response to even minor disturbances. The equipment itself tells a story of escalation. Bulletproof vests have been augmented by ceramic plates capable of stopping high-powered rifle rounds. Handguns have been supplemented, and often replaced, by assault rifles. Tasers, once hailed as less-lethal alternatives, are now deployed with what often appears to be gratuitous frequency, their stunning electrical current a readily accessible tool of compliance. Less visible, but perhaps more impactful, are the sophisticated surveillance technologies, the drones, the license plate readers, the facial recognition software, all designed to monitor and control, creating an omnipresent digital gaze that fosters suspicion rather than trust.

This influx of military hardware and tactics is not merely a superficial aesthetic change; it is a deeply ingrained philosophical shift. The training protocols themselves mirror those of the armed forces, emphasizing tactics of overwhelming force, rapid deployment, and aggressive apprehension. The very language used in police academies and within departments has begun to adopt military terminology: "targets" instead of suspects, "operations" instead of calls for service, "zones of control" instead of neighborhoods. This linguistic conditioning, subtle yet pervasive, shapes the officer's worldview. It fosters a mindset where the community is not a collection of citizens to be served and protected, but a potential enemy territory to be pacified and controlled. The officer, in this new paradigm, is not a servant of the people, but an occupying force, tasked with maintaining order through dominance rather than through dialogue and de-escalation.

The consequences of this militarization are devastatingly tangible. The most immediate impact is the erosion of trust between law enforcement and the communities they are meant to serve. When citizens encounter officers who are heavily armed, armored, and seemingly prepared for combat, it breeds fear, not confidence. The image of a police officer, once a symbol of safety and recourse, becomes associated with aggression and potential violence. This is particularly acute in communities that have historically experienced over-policing and racial bias. For these communities, the sight of military-grade vehicles and heavily armed officers is not a novel development; it is a chilling affirmation of their long-held fears, a stark reminder that they are viewed not as citizens, but as potential threats. The palpable tension that arises from this perceived militarization makes every interaction a potential flashpoint. A simple traffic stop can escalate into a terrifying ordeal. A dispute between neighbors can morph into a scene of overwhelming force. The presumption of innocence is often replaced by a presumption of guilt, and the officer's primary objective shifts from understanding the situation to controlling it, often with brute force.

This "us versus them" mentality, so intrinsic to military operations, creates a chasm between the police and the public. Officers are trained to see themselves as distinct from the civilian population, as a unit apart, tasked with a dangerous mission in often hostile territory. This separation, while perhaps an understandable psychological defense mechanism in actual combat zones, is deeply detrimental in a domestic policing context. It fosters a sense of alienation, where officers may feel unsupported by, and disconnected from, the very people they are sworn to protect. This isolation can lead to a reinforcement of groupthink within departments, making it more difficult to challenge problematic behaviors or to embrace community-oriented policing strategies. The blue wall of silence, a phenomenon often discussed in relation to police misconduct, becomes even more impenetrable when officers view themselves as soldiers in a shared, isolated war.

The adoption of military tactics also fundamentally alters the approach to conflict resolution. De-escalation, the art of diffusing tense situations through communication, empathy, and careful negotiation, is often sidelined in favor of more aggressive, rapid-response strategies. When an officer is equipped with an assault rifle and the tactical training to use it, the temptation to resort to force becomes significantly greater. The emphasis shifts from understanding the root cause of a conflict to neutralizing the perceived threat as quickly and decisively as possible. This can lead to tragic outcomes, where individuals experiencing mental health crises, domestic disputes, or minor infractions are met with a level of force that is disproportionate and ultimately lethal. The officer, trained to subdue and incapacitate, may not possess the nuanced skills necessary to mediate, to listen, or to build rapport. The military model prioritizes mission accomplishment, often at the expense of individual rights and the delicate social fabric of a community.

Furthermore, the infusion of military surplus equipment, often provided through programs like the Department of Defense's 1033 program, has been a significant catalyst in this militarization process. This program allows local law enforcement agencies to acquire excess military equipment, from armored vehicles to M16 rifles, at little to no cost. While ostensibly intended to enhance officer safety and provide essential resources, the long-term consequences have been far more complex and, in many cases, detrimental. The availability of such powerful weaponry and hardware can create a self-perpetuating cycle. Once acquired, the equipment necessitates a change in training and operational philosophy to justify its use. Officers become accustomed to the capabilities of these tools, and the temptation to deploy them, even in situations where they are not strictly necessary, becomes a persistent temptation. This creates a feedback loop where the tools of war are normalized in domestic policing, leading to an increasingly aggressive and adversarial approach to law enforcement.

The psychological impact on officers themselves is also a critical, yet often overlooked, dimension of this militarization. Constantly operating under the assumption that they are in a hostile environment, surrounded by potential threats, can take a significant toll on an officer's mental well-being. The constant need to be vigilant, to be ready for conflict, can lead to hyper-arousal, chronic stress, and a numbing of empathy. When officers are trained to view every encounter as a potential combat situation, it becomes increasingly difficult to engage with individuals on a human level. The capacity for compassion, for understanding, for seeing the person behind the perceived infraction, begins to atrophy.

This can lead to burnout, cynicism, and a detachment from the very community they are tasked with serving. The warrior mindset, while perhaps necessary for survival in an active war zone, is fundamentally incompatible with the principles of community policing and the fundamental role of law enforcement in a democratic society.

The specter of escalating violence is a constant companion to this militarization. When police forces adopt military tactics and equipment, they inherently signal a willingness to use overwhelming force. This can, in turn, provoke a more aggressive response from individuals who feel threatened or cornered. A routine arrest, when conducted with the heavy-handedness of a military raid, can quickly devolve into a violent confrontation. The very presence of heavily armed officers can instill a sense of fear and aggression in the community, leading to an increase in hostility towards police. This creates a dangerous cycle of escalation, where each side responds to the perceived threat from the other with increased force, leading to more injuries, more arrests, and a deeper entrenchment of animosity. The pursuit of order through overwhelming force often results in the very chaos it seeks to prevent, leaving behind a trail of damaged lives and fractured communities.

The subtle shift in the uniform itself is a potent symbol of this transformation. The familiar blue shirt and badge, once emblems of approachable authority, are increasingly being replaced by tactical gear, helmets, and camouflage. While this may provide a degree of protection, it simultaneously creates a visual barrier, signaling a separation from the civilian populace. The officer, when clad in the full regalia of a combat soldier, ceases to be a neighbor, a community member, or a visible representative of civic order. Instead, they become an alien presence, a harbinger of potential conflict, viewed with apprehension rather than with trust. This visual alteration is not merely cosmetic; it is deeply psychological, reinforcing the perception of a police force that is more akin to an occupying army than a trusted guardian. The community, in turn, begins to view their local police not as allies, but as a distant, heavily armed, and potentially hostile entity.

This transformation from officer to enforcer is a chilling testament to how the tools and tactics of war, when imported into domestic law enforcement, can fundamentally undermine the very foundations of community safety and civil liberty. The pursuit of security through militarization often comes at the devastating cost of trust, empathy, and the fundamental human connection that is essential for a healthy and functioning society. The siren's wail, once a call for help, now often signifies the arrival of a force that feels more like an invasion, a stark reminder that the line between protecting and occupying has become dangerously blurred, leaving behind a landscape of fear, suspicion, and escalating aggression. The community, once seen as the object of protection, begins to feel like the adversary, a territory to be managed rather than a populace to be served. This is the grim reality of a police force that has embraced the warrior ethos, trading in its role as community protector for that of a domestic enforcer.

The relentless crucible of law enforcement extracts a heavy toll, a psychological excavation that leaves even the most resilient officers bearing scars unseen. The daily immersion in the raw, often brutal, underbelly of society – witnessing the worst of human behavior, confronting life-and-death situations, and making split-second decisions with profound consequences – grinds down the human spirit. This is not merely a job; it's an existential gauntlet. Yet, in a system that demands unwavering strength and stoicism, the profound psychological cost paid by its agents remains a deeply guarded secret, a silent epidemic festering behind the steely facade of the badge. The absence of robust, readily accessible, and destigmatized mental health support for officers is not just a personal failing of the system; it is a critical, systemic vulnerability that perpetuates the very injustices we seek to dismantle.

Consider the cumulative effect of constant hypervigilance. An officer's nervous system is perpetually on high alert, a finely tuned instrument designed to detect threats in the mundane. Every call, every interaction, carries the implicit risk of sudden violence. This constant state of emergency, this relentless anticipation of danger, rewires the brain. Over time, the body's stress response – the fight-or-flight mechanism – can become dysregulated, leading to chronic anxiety, insomnia, and a pervasive sense of unease that spills over into the officer's personal life. This is not a choice; it is a physiological response to an occupational hazard. When the system fails to acknowledge and address this, it creates a breeding ground for what can manifest as burnout, cynicism, and an emotional numbing that is deeply detrimental to effective policing.

The nature of the work itself exposes officers to a unique constellation of traumatic experiences. They are often the first responders to scenes of horrific accidents, violent crimes, and domestic tragedies. They witness the immediate aftermath of death, the profound grief of families, and the lingering devastation left in the wake of human cruelty. Unlike civilians who may encounter such events sporadically, officers are repeatedly exposed, often in rapid succession. This repeated exposure can lead to Complex Post-Traumatic Stress Disorder (C-PTSD), a condition characterized by more pervasive and enduring symptoms than traditional PTSD, including difficulties with emotional regulation, distorted self-perception, and impaired interpersonal relationships. The inability to process these overwhelming experiences, to compartmentalize and heal, leaves a residue of trauma that can erode an officer's capacity for empathy and sound judgment.

This unaddressed trauma doesn't simply disappear; it festers, manifesting in ways that are profoundly damaging. Burnout becomes a palpable presence, a gnawing exhaustion that saps motivation and enthusiasm. Officers may begin to feel detached, cynical, and increasingly disconnected from their colleagues and the communities they serve. This emotional distance, while perhaps an initial coping mechanism, can calcify into a hardened indifference. When an officer is emotionally depleted and constantly on edge, their ability to de-escalate a tense situation, to engage with individuals with patience and understanding, is severely compromised. The default response can shift from measured problem-solving to reactive force. The very tools and tactics designed to ensure safety can become instruments of excessive force when wielded by someone whose emotional reserves have been depleted by unaddressed trauma.

The concept of "moral injury" is also deeply relevant here. This refers to the psychological distress that results from actions, or the failure to act, that violate one's deeply held moral beliefs. Police officers are often placed in situations where they are forced to make impossible choices, to witness or participate in events that conflict with their sense of right and wrong, or to feel powerless to prevent harm. The internalization of these experiences, without adequate processing and support, can lead to profound guilt, shame, and a sense of moral contamination. This internal conflict can manifest as self-destructive behaviors, substance abuse, and an aggressive posture towards the world as a means of self-protection. The warrior ethos, while sometimes necessary for survival in extreme circumstances, can become a damaging overlay when it clashes with an officer's innate sense of justice and compassion.

Consider the officer responding to a domestic dispute. They arrive at a scene of intense emotional turmoil, where blame is cast, and emotions run high. If this officer is already carrying the weight of past traumas – perhaps a particularly brutal arrest, the death of a partner, or a series of disheartening encounters with the justice system – their perception of the current situation can be significantly distorted. The sounds of shouting might trigger memories of a violent encounter. The perceived defiance of one party might be amplified by a history of feeling disrespected or undermined. Without the emotional regulation skills and support mechanisms to process these triggers, the officer might react with disproportionate aggression, escalating a situation that could have been diffused with calm, measured communication. The absence of mental health support, in this scenario, transforms a potential moment of de-escalation into a pathway towards unnecessary conflict and potential harm.

The culture of law enforcement itself often exacerbates these issues. The stoic, "tough it out" mentality, deeply ingrained in police academies and departmental hierarchies, creates a significant barrier to seeking help. Admitting to mental health struggles is often perceived as a sign of weakness, a career-ending vulnerability. This fear of professional repercussions, coupled with a lack of readily available and confidential resources, leads many officers to suffer in silence. The "blue wall of silence" extends beyond protecting colleagues from accountability; it also encompasses the collective suppression of individual vulnerability. This pervasive stigma means that the very individuals who are trained to help others often feel utterly alone in their own struggles.

The consequences of this systemic neglect are not confined to the individual officer; they have a ripple effect that profoundly impacts the communities they serve. When officers are operating under the weight of untreated trauma, their judgment can be impaired, their decision-making clouded. This can lead to mistakes in procedure, biased enforcement, and, in the most tragic cases, the use of excessive force. The officer who is emotionally detached might fail to recognize the signs of a mental health crisis in a civilian, responding with a heavy hand rather than with compassion and appropriate intervention. The officer who is hypervigilant and distrustful may be quicker to perceive a threat where none exists, leading to unnecessary escalations. The cumulative effect is a breakdown in the very trust that is essential for effective community policing.

The militarization of police, discussed previously, further amplifies the negative consequences of inadequate mental health support. When officers are trained and equipped as soldiers, and when their work is framed as a constant battle against an enemy population, the psychological toll is magnified. The warrior mindset, if not carefully balanced with training in empathy, de-escalation, and a strong understanding of community relations, can become a destructive force. The unaddressed trauma of a "warrior" police officer, operating in what they perceive as hostile territory, is far more likely to translate into aggression and a diminished capacity for human connection than that of an officer who is supported in maintaining a healthy psychological balance. The constant exposure to high-stress, confrontational scenarios, without adequate coping mechanisms, can lead to a cycle of fear, aggression, and dehumanization – on both sides of the badge.

Furthermore, the financial and human cost of ignoring mental health in law enforcement is staggering. Untreated trauma and burnout contribute to higher rates of divorce, substance abuse, and suicide among officers. The emotional toll on their families is immense, creating a secondary layer of suffering. Beyond the personal tragedies, there are significant costs to departments and taxpayers: increased sick leave, higher turnover rates, expensive litigation stemming from officer misconduct, and the immeasurable cost of damaged community relations. Investing in comprehensive mental health support is not merely a compassionate endeavor; it is a pragmatic necessity for the long-term health and effectiveness of law enforcement agencies and the well-being of the communities they are sworn to protect.

The current approach, which often relies on reactive measures or voluntary, often underfunded, employee assistance programs, is woefully insufficient. There needs to be a proactive, integrated, and destigmatized system of mental health care embedded within law enforcement agencies. This includes regular psychological evaluations, accessible counseling services that are strictly confidential, peer support programs, and specialized training for officers and supervisors on recognizing and addressing the signs of psychological distress. Critically, this support must extend beyond the active duty years, acknowledging the long-term impact of the job on an officer's mental well-being even after they have hung up their badge.

The absence of adequate mental health support is a profound systemic failure, a dark undercurrent that compromises the integrity of the justice system from within. It creates a dangerous feedback loop where the psychological wounds of officers, left unaddressed, contribute to the very societal problems they are meant to resolve. The inability to heal from trauma, to manage the relentless stress, and to overcome the ingrained stigma associated with seeking help, not only endangers the officers themselves but also erodes the quality of justice dispensed and the fundamental trust between law enforcement and the public. Until the psychological well-being of officers is treated as a critical component of public safety, the pursuit of true justice will remain an elusive ideal, forever shadowed by the unseen battles fought within the minds of those who wear the badge. The empathy deficit that plagues the system, the willingness to deploy overwhelming force rather than seek understanding, can be directly traced, in part, to this profound neglect of the human beings behind the uniforms. They are not invulnerable; they are, in fact, uniquely vulnerable to the psychological ravages of their profession, and the system's failure to provide adequate care is a betrayal of both the officer and the citizen.

The American justice system, for all its intricate machinery and imposing pronouncements, often operates within a narrow, retributive framework. It is a system built on the premise of punishment, of societal reprisal for transgressions. The scales of justice are too frequently weighted towards imposing penalties, towards isolating individuals and branding them as irredeemable. This punitive approach, while appearing to offer a clear-cut solution, fundamentally misses the mark. It addresses the *act* of wrongdoing, but rarely delves into the *causes* or the *consequences* in a way that fosters genuine healing or prevents future harm. The focus remains stubbornly on the past offense, rather than on the future potential for change, understanding, and reconciliation. This is where the sterile, often dehumanizing, machinery of traditional justice encounters its greatest limitations, particularly when viewed through the lens of an empathy deficit that permeates the system.

However, a compelling counter-narrative is emerging, a whisper of hope in the clamor for more effective and humane approaches. This alternative, known as restorative justice, offers a profound paradigm shift. It moves away from the adversarial courtroom and towards a more collaborative, community-centered model. Instead of asking, "What law was broken, who broke it, and what punishment do they deserve?", restorative justice asks, "Who has been harmed, what are their needs, and whose obligation is it to meet those needs?" This seemingly simple reframing has transformative implications, injecting a vital element of empathy and human connection into a system often characterized by its cold, impersonal nature. It acknowledges that crime is not merely an abstract violation of law, but a rupture in the fabric of human relationships and community trust.

The core of restorative justice lies in its emphasis on repairing harm. This isn't about excusing or downplaying the offense; rather, it's about actively addressing the wounds inflicted. For victims, this can mean finally having their voice heard, understanding the impact of the crime on their lives, and having a say in how the harm can be mended. This is a stark contrast to the often-passive role victims play in traditional proceedings, where they can feel re-traumatized by the legal process itself, reduced to witnesses in a drama that unfolds without their full agency. Restorative practices create a space for dialogue, allowing victims to express their pain, ask questions of the offender, and articulate what they need to begin the healing process. This can involve anything from apologies and financial restitution to community service or symbolic gestures of reconciliation. The goal is empowerment and validation, recognizing the victim's humanity and their right to be made whole again.

Equally crucial is the focus on offender accountability, but not accountability in the purely punitive sense. Restorative justice seeks

transformative accountability, where the offender is not merely punished but is actively encouraged to understand the full impact of their actions, to take responsibility for the harm they have caused, and to make amends. This often involves direct encounters with the victim or their representatives, facilitated by trained mediators. These dialogues can be intensely challenging, forcing offenders to confront the human cost of their choices in a way that abstract legal judgments often fail to do. The process is designed to foster empathy, to move the offender beyond justifications and defenses towards genuine remorse and a commitment to behavioral change. It recognizes that true accountability comes not from coercion, but from a deep, internal understanding of one's wrongdoing and a willingness to rectify it.

The community also plays a vital role in restorative justice models. Crime does not occur in a vacuum; it impacts families, neighborhoods, and society at large. Restorative processes often involve community members, elders, or support networks, providing a broader perspective and a supportive environment for both victim and offender. This collective involvement reinforces the idea that justice is a shared responsibility and that the community has a stake in preventing future harm and fostering a safer, more cohesive environment. It's about rebuilding trust, restoring relationships, and strengthening the social bonds that crime so often erodes. By bringing people together, it counters the isolating effects of crime and promotes a sense of shared responsibility for well-being.

Consider the power of a properly facilitated victim-offender mediation. Imagine a young person who has committed a burglary, leaving a family feeling violated and unsafe in their own home. In a traditional courtroom, the outcome might be incarceration, a sterile judgment that offers little solace to the family and potentially hardens the offender. In a restorative justice setting, the victim and offender might sit down together, perhaps with a mediator present. The victim can describe the fear they experienced, the disruption to their lives, the feeling of violated sanctuary. The offender, confronted with the tangible human impact of their actions, may begin to grasp the gravity of what they've done beyond the legal infraction. They might offer a sincere apology, commit to repaying the stolen items or their value, and perhaps even engage in community service that benefits the neighborhood. This process doesn't erase the crime, but it transforms the experience of it, offering a path towards healing for the victim and a meaningful opportunity for the offender to learn and contribute positively to society. The encounter is not about punishment; it is about recognition, responsibility, and repair.

This stands in stark contrast to the often-impersonal and dehumanizing nature of the traditional justice system. The vastness of court dockets, the legalistic jargon, and the inherent adversarial nature can leave all parties feeling unheard and alienated. Victims can feel like props in a legal drama, their trauma reduced to evidence. Offenders can feel like nameless statistics, their humanity stripped away by the machinery of the state. This is where the empathy deficit becomes most glaringly apparent. The system is designed to process cases, not necessarily to process people or their pain. Restorative justice, by contrast, prioritizes the human element. It creates a space for genuine connection, understanding, and the acknowledgement of shared humanity, even in the face of wrongdoing.

The benefits of restorative justice extend beyond individual cases. By fostering a sense of shared responsibility and by addressing the root causes of crime, these models can contribute to lower recidivism rates and stronger, more resilient communities. When offenders are given the opportunity to make amends and to reintegrate into society as responsible citizens, rather than being perpetually stigmatized, the entire community benefits. It's a proactive approach that aims to break cycles of violence and offending, rather than simply managing their symptoms through incarceration. It's an investment in human potential, recognizing that individuals are capable of change and that communities are stronger when they work together to heal and to prevent harm.

Furthermore, the implementation of restorative justice principles can serve as a powerful antidote to the cynicism and disillusionment that can afflict both victims and offenders within the traditional system. For victims, it offers a sense of agency and validation that is often missing. For offenders, it provides a pathway to redemption and a chance to regain their dignity, not by escaping responsibility, but by embracing it in a constructive manner. This can be particularly impactful for young offenders, where early intervention through restorative practices can steer them away from a life of crime and towards positive engagement with society. It's about offering a second chance, not as a handout, but as a consequence of genuine remorse and a commitment to making things right.

The challenge, of course, lies in its widespread adoption and effective implementation. Restorative justice requires skilled facilitators, dedicated resources, and a willingness to move beyond deeply ingrained punitive impulses. It demands a cultural shift within the justice system and within society at large. It necessitates a commitment to understanding that true justice involves more than just retribution; it involves healing, reconciliation, and the rebuilding of communities. This is not to suggest that punitive measures have no place, but rather that they should not be the sole or even primary response. They should be integrated into a broader framework that prioritizes restorative principles whenever possible.

The potential for restorative justice to humanize the justice system is immense. It offers a path forward from a system that often perpetuates cycles of harm and alienation, towards one that fosters understanding, accountability, and genuine healing. It recognizes that every individual, regardless of their actions, is a human being, and that the justice system has a responsibility to treat them as such. By focusing on repairing harm, empowering victims, and fostering transformative accountability for offenders, restorative justice models provide a powerful and compassionate alternative, a testament to the enduring power of empathy in the pursuit of a more just and humane society. It is a beacon of hope, illuminating a less punitive and more restorative future for the American justice system, one that acknowledges the profound human cost of crime and seeks to mend rather than merely to punish. The quiet work of victim-offender dialogues, community conferencing, and circle processes, often happening on the fringes of the formal legal system, represents a profound reorientation of what justice can and should be. It is a tangible manifestation of the humanizing factor, a conscious effort to infuse empathy into a system that has too often been starved of it, offering a compelling vision of a justice system that seeks not only to punish but to heal and to restore. The narrative of justice, too often a story of condemnation and isolation, can become a story of understanding, responsibility, and ultimately, of reintegration and renewed community.

The sterile efficiency of the justice system, while aiming for impartial application of law, has, in its pursuit of order, often inadvertently erected walls between those tasked with upholding it and the very communities they serve. This divide, a chasm of mistrust and misunderstanding, is a breeding ground for the empathy deficit that we've explored. It is a deficit that allows for the dehumanization of both the offender and, at times, the victim, reducing complex human experiences to mere case files and statistical probabilities. But what if the solution lies not in more complex legal frameworks or harsher penalties, but in a fundamental reorientation of how law enforcement interacts with the public? What if the pathway to genuine safety and a more empathetic justice system begins on the streets, not just in the courtroom, but in the everyday interactions between police officers and the people they are sworn to protect? This is the realm of community-oriented policing, a philosophy that seeks to bridge that divide, to rebuild fractured trust, and to foster a shared sense of responsibility for public safety.

Community-oriented policing, at its heart, is a proactive strategy that moves law enforcement away from a purely reactive, incident-driven model. Instead of simply responding to calls for service – the burglaries, the assaults, the disturbances – it emphasizes the importance of building sustained relationships with the residents of a community. This isn't about officers as mere enforcers, but as integral members of the neighborhood, invested in its well-being and its future. It's about officers walking the beat, getting to know the shopkeepers, the parents waiting for school buses, the elderly residents on their porches. It's about being visible, accessible, and approachable, transforming the uniform from a symbol of authority and potential threat into one of partnership and support. This shift in perception is crucial; it's the first step in dismantling the adversarial stance that so often characterizes the relationship between police and the public, particularly in marginalized communities where historical grievances and experiences of biased policing have created deep-seated distrust.

The success of community-oriented policing hinges on fostering trust. Without trust, any attempt at partnership is superficial, a veneer of cooperation that crumbles at the first sign of trouble. Building trust is a slow, painstaking process, often involving countless small gestures and consistent, reliable actions. It means engaging in dialogue, not just dispensing directives. It means listening to residents' concerns, even if they seem minor or outside the immediate scope of criminal activity. It means understanding that a broken streetlamp or a lack of youth programs can be as detrimental to a community's safety and well-being as a street crime. These are the "broken windows" of social infrastructure, and addressing them collaboratively with residents can prevent more serious problems from taking root. Imagine an officer who takes the time to learn the names of the children in a local park, who stops to chat with a group of teenagers about their aspirations, or who attends a neighborhood watch meeting not to issue warnings, but to genuinely solicit input. These interactions, seemingly small, accumulate over time, building a reservoir of goodwill and a sense that the police are truly on their side, invested in the community's collective success.

One of the most powerful aspects of community-oriented policing is its focus on addressing the root causes of crime, rather than simply treating its symptoms. Traditional policing often deals with the immediate fallout of social and economic distress – drug-related offenses, property crimes, public disturbances. These are often manifestations of deeper issues: poverty, lack of educational opportunities, mental health challenges, lack of affordable housing, and systemic discrimination. Community policing initiatives recognize this reality and seek to work

with residents and other community stakeholders – schools, social service agencies, local businesses, faith-based organizations – to tackle these underlying problems. This might involve establishing youth mentorship programs, partnering with mental health professionals to respond to crisis situations, or working with city planners to improve community infrastructure. It's a holistic approach that acknowledges that public safety is not solely the responsibility of the police, but a shared endeavor that requires a multifaceted strategy.

Consider the example of a neighborhood struggling with a surge in petty theft and vandalism. A purely reactive police response might involve increased patrols and more arrests, which can be costly, contribute to jail overcrowding, and do little to address the underlying issues driving the behavior. In a community-oriented model, however, officers would engage with residents to understand the specific circumstances. Are the thefts occurring because families are struggling to afford basic necessities? Is the vandalism a symptom of boredom and a lack of recreational activities for young people? By collaborating with local charities, schools, and community centers, police can help facilitate programs that provide job training, after-school tutoring, or safe spaces for teenagers. They might also work with businesses to implement better lighting or security measures, or organize community clean-up days that foster a sense of shared ownership and pride. This approach not only aims to reduce crime but also to build a stronger, more resilient community, addressing the grievances that might otherwise fester and lead to further conflict.

The success of these initiatives often lies in their ability to empower residents. When people feel they have a voice, that their concerns are heard and acted upon, they are more likely to become active participants in ensuring their own safety. Neighborhood watch programs, when properly supported and integrated with police efforts, can be incredibly effective. These are not vigilante groups; they are trained residents who serve as extra eyes and ears for law enforcement, reporting suspicious activity and fostering a sense of collective vigilance. This collaborative model distributes the burden of maintaining public safety, allowing police resources to be deployed more strategically and effectively. It shifts the paradigm from a top-down enforcement model to one of genuine partnership, where the community is an active agent in its own protection.

There are numerous real-world examples that illustrate the power of this approach. In many cities, specialized units have been established where officers are specifically trained in de-escalation techniques, crisis intervention, and community engagement. These officers are not just responding to calls; they are building relationships with community leaders, attending local events, and working proactively to identify and address potential conflicts before they erupt. Their focus is on problem-solving, not just law enforcement. For instance, a long-standing issue with gang activity in a particular neighborhood might be addressed not just through arrests, but through a coordinated effort involving police, social workers, schools, and community outreach programs. Officers might work with local youth centers to provide positive alternatives for at-risk young people, mentor them, and connect them with educational and employment opportunities. This integrated approach acknowledges that the causes of gang involvement are complex and require a response that goes far beyond simply increasing police presence.

The development of "community policing liaisons" or "beat officers" who are assigned to specific neighborhoods and remain there for extended periods can also be incredibly effective. This continuity allows officers to develop a deep understanding of the community's unique dynamics, its challenges, and its strengths. They become familiar faces, people that residents can approach with confidence, knowing they will be met with understanding and a genuine desire to help. This familiarity breeds familiarity, and familiarity, in turn, fosters trust. It's a stark contrast to the constant rotation of officers that can leave communities feeling like they are perpetually dealing with strangers who lack a nuanced understanding of their lived realities.

Moreover, community-oriented policing can be a powerful tool in dismantling the perception of police as an occupying force, particularly in communities that have historically experienced over-policing and discriminatory practices. By actively engaging with residents, soliciting feedback, and demonstrating a commitment to fairness and accountability, police departments can begin to repair these damaged relationships. This requires a genuine willingness to listen to criticism, to acknowledge past mistakes, and to implement reforms that address systemic issues of bias and misconduct. It's not enough to simply say "we are here to help"; that message must be backed up by tangible actions that demonstrate a commitment to serving all members of the community equitably.

The challenge, of course, lies in implementing these strategies effectively and sustainably. It requires a significant investment in training, resources, and a fundamental shift in departmental culture. It means moving away from a purely statistics-driven approach to policing, where arrests and citations are the primary metrics of success, towards one that values relationship-building, problem-solving, and community satisfaction. It also means ensuring that officers have the autonomy and support to engage in these community-focused activities, rather than being solely focused on responding to the next emergency call. This often involves rethinking staffing models and patrol strategies to allow for more proactive community engagement.

Furthermore, the success of community policing is not solely dependent on the actions of law enforcement. It requires active participation and collaboration from the community itself. Residents must be willing to engage with the police, to share information, and to work together to find solutions. This is a reciprocal relationship, and its effectiveness relies on the willingness of both sides to invest in building bridges and fostering mutual respect. When this partnership flourishes, it creates a virtuous cycle: increased trust leads to greater cooperation, which leads to more effective problem-solving, which in turn further strengthens trust and reinforces the sense of shared responsibility for public safety.

The impact of this approach on the broader justice system is profound. When communities feel safer and more connected to their law enforcement, the conditions that often lead to crime are mitigated. Fewer incidents mean fewer arrests, fewer court cases, and a reduced burden on the judicial system. More importantly, it fosters an environment where the principles of restorative justice can take root and flourish. When victims and offenders are part of a community that is actively engaged in addressing harm and promoting healing, the potential for genuine reconciliation and reintegration increases exponentially. The empathy deficit, so prevalent in a system that often isolates individuals and divorces them from their social context, begins to shrink when the human face of justice is visible on every corner, engaged in genuine dialogue and collaboration. It's a vision of a justice system that is not just about punishment and retribution, but about building stronger, safer, and more compassionate communities from the ground up, one relationship at a time. The true measure of public safety, in this model, is not the number of arrests, but the quality of life and the strength of the bonds that hold a community together.

The sterile efficiency of the justice system, while aiming for impartial application of law, has, in its pursuit of order, often inadvertently erected walls between those tasked with upholding it and the very communities they serve. This divide, a chasm of mistrust and misunderstanding, is a breeding ground for the empathy deficit that we've explored. It is a deficit that allows for the dehumanization of both the offender and, at times, the victim, reducing complex human experiences to mere case files and statistical probabilities. But what if the solution lies not in more complex legal frameworks or harsher penalties, but in a fundamental reorientation of how law enforcement interacts with the public? What if the pathway to genuine safety and a more empathetic justice system begins on the streets, not just in the courtroom, but in the everyday interactions between police officers and the people they are sworn to protect? This is the realm of community-oriented policing, a philosophy that seeks to bridge that divide, to rebuild fractured trust, and to foster a shared sense of responsibility for public safety.

Community-oriented policing, at its heart, is a proactive strategy that moves law enforcement away from a purely reactive, incident-driven model. Instead of simply responding to calls for service – the burglaries, the assaults, the disturbances – it emphasizes the importance of building sustained relationships with the residents of a community. This isn't about officers as mere enforcers, but as integral members of the neighborhood, invested in its well-being and its future. It's about officers walking the beat, getting to know the shopkeepers, the parents waiting for school buses, the elderly residents on their porches. It's about being visible, accessible, and approachable, transforming the uniform from a symbol of authority and potential threat into one of partnership and support. This shift in perception is crucial; it's the first step in dismantling the adversarial stance that so often characterizes the relationship between police and the public, particularly in marginalized communities where historical grievances and experiences of biased policing have created deep-seated distrust.

The success of community-oriented policing hinges on fostering trust. Without trust, any attempt at partnership is superficial, a veneer of cooperation that crumbles at the first sign of trouble. Building trust is a slow, painstaking process, often involving countless small gestures and consistent, reliable actions. It means engaging in dialogue, not just dispensing directives. It means listening to residents' concerns, even if they seem minor or outside the immediate scope of criminal activity. It means understanding that a broken streetlamp or a lack of youth programs can be as detrimental to a community's safety and well-being as a street crime. These are the "broken windows" of social infrastructure, and addressing them collaboratively with residents can prevent more serious problems from taking root. Imagine an officer who takes the time to learn the names of the children in a local park, who stops to chat with a group of teenagers about their aspirations, or who attends a neighborhood watch meeting not to issue warnings, but to genuinely solicit input. These interactions, seemingly small, accumulate over time, building a reservoir of goodwill and a sense that the police are truly on their side, invested in the community's collective success.

One of the most powerful aspects of community-oriented policing is its focus on addressing the root causes of crime, rather than simply treating its symptoms. Traditional policing often deals with the immediate fallout of social and economic distress – drug-related offenses, property crimes, public disturbances. These are often manifestations of deeper issues: poverty, lack of educational opportunities, mental health challenges, lack of affordable housing, and systemic discrimination. Community policing initiatives recognize this reality and seek to work

with residents and other community stakeholders – schools, social service agencies, local businesses, faith-based organizations – to tackle these underlying problems. This might involve establishing youth mentorship programs, partnering with mental health professionals to respond to crisis situations, or working with city planners to improve community infrastructure. It's a holistic approach that acknowledges that public safety is not solely the responsibility of the police, but a shared endeavor that requires a multifaceted strategy.

Consider the example of a neighborhood struggling with a surge in petty theft and vandalism. A purely reactive police response might involve increased patrols and more arrests, which can be costly, contribute to jail overcrowding, and do little to address the underlying issues driving the behavior. In a community-oriented model, however, officers would engage with residents to understand the specific circumstances. Are the thefts occurring because families are struggling to afford basic necessities? Is the vandalism a symptom of boredom and a lack of recreational activities for young people? By collaborating with local charities, schools, and community centers, police can help facilitate programs that provide job training, after-school tutoring, or safe spaces for teenagers. They might also work with businesses to implement better lighting or security measures, or organize community clean-up days that foster a sense of shared ownership and pride. This approach not only aims to reduce crime but also to build a stronger, more resilient community, addressing the grievances that might otherwise fester and lead to further conflict.

The success of these initiatives often lies in their ability to empower residents. When people feel they have a voice, that their concerns are heard and acted upon, they are more likely to become active participants in ensuring their own safety. Neighborhood watch programs, when properly supported and integrated with police efforts, can be incredibly effective. These are not vigilante groups; they are trained residents who serve as extra eyes and ears for law enforcement, reporting suspicious activity and fostering a sense of collective vigilance. This collaborative model distributes the burden of maintaining public safety, allowing police resources to be deployed more strategically and effectively. It shifts the paradigm from a top-down enforcement model to one of genuine partnership, where the community is an active agent in its own protection.

There are numerous real-world examples that illustrate the power of this approach. In many cities, specialized units have been established where officers are specifically trained in de-escalation techniques, crisis intervention, and community engagement. These officers are not just responding to calls; they are building relationships with community leaders, attending local events, and working proactively to identify and address potential conflicts before they erupt. Their focus is on problem-solving, not just law enforcement. For instance, a long-standing issue with gang activity in a particular neighborhood might be addressed not just through arrests, but through a coordinated effort involving police, social workers, schools, and community outreach programs. Officers might work with local youth centers to provide positive alternatives for at-risk young people, mentor them, and connect them with educational and employment opportunities. This integrated approach acknowledges that the causes of gang involvement are complex and require a response that goes far beyond simply increasing police presence.

The development of "community policing liaisons" or "beat officers" who are assigned to specific neighborhoods and remain there for extended periods can also be incredibly effective. This continuity allows officers to develop a deep understanding of the community's unique dynamics, its challenges, and its strengths. They become familiar faces, people that residents can approach with confidence, knowing they will be met with understanding and a genuine desire to help. This familiarity breeds familiarity, and familiarity, in turn, fosters trust. It's a stark contrast to the constant rotation of officers that can leave communities feeling like they are perpetually dealing with strangers who lack a nuanced understanding of their lived realities.

Moreover, community-oriented policing can be a powerful tool in dismantling the perception of police as an occupying force, particularly in communities that have historically experienced over-policing and discriminatory practices. By actively engaging with residents, soliciting feedback, and demonstrating a commitment to fairness and accountability, police departments can begin to repair these damaged relationships. This requires a genuine willingness to listen to criticism, to acknowledge past mistakes, and to implement reforms that address systemic issues of bias and misconduct. It's not enough to simply say "we are here to help"; that message must be backed up by tangible actions that demonstrate a commitment to serving all members of the community equitably.

The challenge, of course, lies in implementing these strategies effectively and sustainably. It requires a significant investment in training, resources, and a fundamental shift in departmental culture. It means moving away from a purely statistics-driven approach to policing, where arrests and citations are the primary metrics of success, towards one that values relationship-building, problem-solving, and community satisfaction. It also means ensuring that officers have the autonomy and support to engage in these community-focused activities, rather than being solely focused on responding to the next emergency call. This often involves rethinking staffing models and patrol strategies to allow for more proactive community engagement.

Furthermore, the success of community policing is not solely dependent on the actions of law enforcement. It requires active participation and collaboration from the community itself. Residents must be willing to engage with the police, to share information, and to work together to find solutions. This is a reciprocal relationship, and its effectiveness relies on the willingness of both sides to invest in building bridges and fostering mutual respect. When this partnership flourishes, it creates a virtuous cycle: increased trust leads to greater cooperation, which leads to more effective problem-solving, which in turn further strengthens trust and reinforces the sense of shared responsibility for public safety.

The impact of this approach on the broader justice system is profound. When communities feel safer and more connected to their law enforcement, the conditions that often lead to crime are mitigated. Fewer incidents mean fewer arrests, fewer court cases, and a reduced burden on the judicial system. More importantly, it fosters an environment where the principles of restorative justice can take root and flourish. When victims and offenders are part of a community that is actively engaged in addressing harm and promoting healing, the potential for genuine reconciliation and reintegration increases exponentially. The empathy deficit, so prevalent in a system that often isolates individuals and divorces them from their social context, begins to shrink when the human face of justice is visible on every corner, engaged in genuine dialogue and collaboration. It's a vision of a justice system that is not just about punishment and retribution, but about building stronger, safer, and more compassionate communities from the ground up, one relationship at a time. The true measure of public safety, in this model, is not the number of arrests, but the quality of life and the strength of the bonds that hold a community together.

The preceding exploration of community-oriented policing reveals a critical truth: at the heart of a failing justice system lies a profound deficit, not of resources or regulations, but of something far more fundamental – empathy. This isn't about sentimentality; it's about the capacity to understand, to connect with, and to care about the human beings who populate our streets, our neighborhoods, and our courtrooms. Without this essential ingredient, the machinery of justice, however well-oiled and technically proficient, grinds to a halt, becoming a cold, impersonal, and ultimately oppressive force. The absence of what could broadly be termed 'love' – not romantic love, but a deep-seated compassion, a recognition of shared humanity, and a commitment to the interconnectedness of all individuals within a society – is the root cause of the insidious 'tyranny tax' that burdens our communities.

When empathy is absent, individuals are reduced. The person accused of a crime becomes a case number, a set of behaviors to be cataloged and judged, rather than a complex individual shaped by a lifetime of experiences, influences, and perhaps, profound suffering. The victim, too, can be dehumanized, their trauma distilled into a statistic or a justification for punitive action, rather than being seen as a whole person whose pain demands genuine understanding and a path towards healing. This detachment allows for decisions to be made that, while perhaps legally sound, are morally bankrupt, perpetuating cycles of harm and alienation. The system, in its quest for objective impartiality, paradoxically becomes deeply subjective, reflecting the biases and blind spots of those within it, precisely because it has lost touch with the human element.

Consider the implications of this empathy deficit on the very fabric of our neighborhoods. When law enforcement officers are viewed solely as agents of enforcement, their presence can be perceived as an imposition, a force external to the community, rather than a part of it. This perception, often born from historical injustices and experiences of profiling and excessive force, breeds fear and resentment. The interaction, which should ideally be one of service and protection, becomes a tense negotiation of power, where communication is stunted and understanding is impossible. This creates fertile ground for the 'tyranny tax' to flourish – the unacknowledged cost borne by communities in the form of fractured trust, heightened anxiety, and a pervasive sense of injustice. This tax is paid in lost potential, in diminished civic engagement, and in the erosion of social cohesion.

The concept of 'love' as a driving force within the justice system is not a naive ideal; it is a pragmatic recognition of the necessity for human connection to foster accountability and facilitate genuine rehabilitation. When the system operates without this animating principle, it becomes a blunt instrument, focused on retribution rather than restoration. The punitive measures, however severe, often fail to address the underlying issues that lead to criminal behavior. A person incarcerated without any genuine attempt to understand their circumstances, their motivations, or their potential for change is likely to emerge from the system hardened, embittered, and ill-equipped to reintegrate into society. The cycle of recidivism, therefore, becomes an almost inevitable consequence of a system that lacks the capacity for compassion.

The 'tyranny tax' manifests in myriad ways, often subtly, but always detrimentally. It is the disproportionate incarceration rates of certain demographics, a direct result of systemic biases that are allowed to persist because the individuals making decisions lack the empathetic lens to recognize their impact. It is the routine use of excessive force, often employed against individuals perceived as 'other' or 'dangerous,' without sufficient consideration for their vulnerability or the potential for de-escalation. It is the pervasive fear that prevents individuals from reporting crimes or cooperating with investigations, because they anticipate being treated with suspicion or indifference rather than support. This pervasive lack of care creates a self-perpetuating cycle of disadvantage and marginalization.

The absence of empathy also infects the internal culture of law enforcement and judicial institutions. When officers are trained and rewarded based solely on metrics of arrests and convictions, the emphasis shifts from serving and protecting to containing and controlling. The human stories behind the statistics are ignored, and the emotional toll of constant exposure to trauma and conflict is left unaddressed. This can lead to burnout, cynicism, and a gradual erosion of the very qualities that make for effective and compassionate policing. The individual officer, overwhelmed by the demands of the job and stripped of the emotional resources to connect with the people they serve, can become as much a victim of the empathy deficit as the community itself.

To truly dismantle the 'tyranny tax,' we must cultivate a justice system that is imbued with a sense of profound humanistic concern. This begins with acknowledging that every individual, regardless of their past actions, is a human being deserving of respect and dignity. It means prioritizing the well-being of communities, understanding that true safety is built on trust and collaboration, not coercion and fear. It requires a deliberate and sustained effort to foster empathy at every level of the system, from the training academies to the highest courts. This is not a call for a system that excuses wrongdoing or abandons accountability, but for one that recognizes that accountability can and should be pursued through means that are both just and humane.

The path forward necessitates a radical shift in our understanding of what constitutes effective justice. It means moving beyond a purely punitive model and embracing approaches that prioritize healing, reconciliation, and the restoration of dignity. Restorative justice practices, for example, offer a powerful framework for addressing harm by bringing together victims, offenders, and community members to collaboratively find solutions that promote understanding and repair relationships. These approaches, by their very nature, demand empathy, requiring individuals to step into each other's shoes, to listen to each other's stories, and to recognize their shared humanity.

Furthermore, the institutions of justice must actively work to dismantle the structural barriers that perpetuate the empathy deficit. This includes reforming recruitment and training practices to attract and develop individuals who possess strong interpersonal skills and a genuine commitment to public service. It means creating environments within law enforcement agencies and the courts that encourage open dialogue, critical self-reflection, and a willingness to learn from mistakes. Accountability mechanisms must be strengthened, not just to punish misconduct, but to ensure that the system is responsive to the needs and concerns of the communities it serves.

The 'tyranny tax' is not an inevitable byproduct of societal order; it is a consequence of a system that has, in its pursuit of control, forgotten its fundamental purpose: to serve and protect all members of society with fairness and compassion. Reclaiming this purpose requires a conscious and unwavering commitment to cultivating empathy, to fostering a sense of interconnectedness, and to recognizing that the true measure of a just society lies not in the number of people it punishes, but in the number of people it empowers to thrive. Without this fundamental reorientation, the walls of indifference will continue to rise, and the 'tyranny tax' will continue to be levied, extracting a devastating toll on individuals and communities alike. The absence of love, in its broadest sense of humanistic concern and interconnectedness, renders the system incapable of delivering true justice.

Chapter 4: Reclaiming Your Rights

The moment an officer approaches your vehicle, or knocks on your door, a silent alarm should begin to sound in your mind, not one of panic, but of preparedness. This isn't about being confrontational; it's about being informed. Understanding your fundamental rights under the United States Constitution is not merely a legal formality; it is your first and most potent line of defense against the potential for overreach, misunderstanding, or outright injustice within the legal system. These rights, enshrined in the Bill of Rights, are not privileges to be granted or withheld by law enforcement; they are inherent, existing the moment you are engaged by an officer of the state. To neglect them is to disarm yourself in a situation where knowledge is your primary weapon.

The most universally recognized, and perhaps the most critical, of these rights is your protection against unreasonable searches and seizures, guaranteed by the Fourth Amendment. This amendment dictates that law enforcement officers must have probable cause to believe that a crime has been committed or is about to be committed to legally stop and search you, your property, or your vehicle. They cannot simply demand to search your car because they "have a feeling" or because you appear "suspicious." While the definition of "suspicious" can be alarmingly broad in practice, the legal standard remains probable cause. This means they need specific, articulable facts that would lead a reasonable person to believe evidence of a crime will be found. If an officer asks to search your vehicle, and you have not committed any traffic violations or displayed any behavior that would constitute probable cause, you have the right to refuse that search. Simply stating, "Officer, I do not consent to a search of my vehicle," is a clear and legally sound response. It is vital to remain calm and polite when doing so. An aggressive or defiant tone can escalate a situation, but a calm refusal is your right, and exercising it does not, in itself, create probable cause. Many people mistakenly believe that refusing a search is an admission of guilt. This is fundamentally untrue. Refusal is merely the assertion of a constitutional right. It is crucial to remember that while you can refuse a search, an officer who has established probable cause, or has a warrant, can proceed with the search regardless of your consent. The distinction lies in the legality of their actions.

Beyond the Fourth Amendment, the Fifth Amendment provides critical protections during any interaction that might lead to your detention or arrest, most notably the right to remain silent. This right, famously invoked with the phrase "You have the right to remain silent. Anything you say can and will be used against you in a court of law. You have the right to an attorney. If you cannot afford an attorney, one will be provided for you," is not just for those being formally arrested. It extends to any situation where you are not free to leave, a concept known as being "in custody." Even during a routine traffic stop, if the interaction moves beyond issuing a ticket and towards a potential criminal investigation, you are effectively in custody. This means you have the right to stop talking to the officer at any point. It is often wise to do so immediately after identifying yourself and providing your driver's license and registration. Any further questioning about your whereabouts, your activities, or your associations can potentially be used to build a case against you. Do not feel obligated to "explain yourself" or "clear your name" by talking. The burden of proof lies with the prosecution, not with you. The impulse to be helpful, to reassure the officer of your innocence, or to offer details you believe will exonerate you, can often backfire spectacularly. Innocent explanations can be misinterpreted, taken out of context, or twisted to appear incriminating. A simple, polite, "Officer, I wish to remain silent," or "I am not going to answer any questions without my attorney present," is a complete and constitutionally protected response.

The Sixth Amendment further bolsters your protections by guaranteeing the right to legal counsel. This right is not limited to the courtroom. You have the right to have an attorney present during any custodial interrogation. If you are being questioned by law enforcement and you invoke your right to an attorney, all questioning must cease until your lawyer is present. This is a critical safeguard. An attorney is trained to navigate the legal complexities of questioning, to protect your rights, and to ensure that any statements you make are not used against you. Do not feel ashamed or embarrassed to request an attorney. It is a sign of your understanding of your rights and a responsible step in protecting yourself. Many individuals, particularly those from marginalized communities who may have had negative past experiences with law enforcement, harbor a deep-seated distrust of the legal system. This distrust, while often rooted in valid historical grievances, can paradoxically lead them to believe that invoking their rights is a sign of guilt or will somehow antagonize the authorities further. This is a dangerous misconception. Exercising your constitutional rights is a sign of civic responsibility and self-preservation, not an act of defiance.

The practical application of these rights often begins with the traffic stop. While many stops are routine and end with a warning or a ticket, they can quickly escalate. When an officer approaches your vehicle, they may ask for your license and registration. You are generally required to produce these documents. However, beyond that, you are not obligated to answer further questions. If the officer asks, "Where are you coming from?" or "What have you been doing tonight?" you have the right to decline to answer. A polite "I'm not going to answer that question, Officer" is sufficient. If the officer then asks to search your vehicle, remember your Fourth Amendment rights. "Officer, I do not consent to a search." If they proceed to search anyway, do not resist physically. Make your objection known clearly: "Officer, I do not consent to this search, but I am not going to physically resist." This is crucial. Physical resistance can lead to charges of assault or resisting arrest, which can have severe consequences and complicate your legal situation immensely, regardless of the legality of the initial search. Your safety and freedom from unwarranted physical confrontation are paramount.

It is also important to understand what constitutes "custody." This is not always as clear-cut as an arrest. If a reasonable person in your situation would not feel free to leave, you are considered to be in custody. This can occur during a stop on the street where an officer is detaining you for questioning. If you are unsure whether you are free to leave, you can politely ask, "Officer, am I free to leave?" If the answer is yes, you can calmly walk away. If the answer is no, or if the officer indicates you are being detained, then your right to remain silent and your right to an attorney become immediately relevant. Do not attempt to engage in a debate about whether you are in custody. Simply state your desire to remain silent and your request for an attorney.

Interrogations, whether at the police station or at your home, are where the Fifth Amendment right to remain silent and the Sixth Amendment right to counsel are most critical. If law enforcement comes to your home and asks to speak with you, you are not obligated to let them in without a warrant. You can politely state, "I am not going to invite you in without a warrant." If they present a warrant, you must allow them entry, but your rights to remain silent and to have an attorney present during any questioning still apply. Never assume that because they have a warrant to search your home, they also have the right to question you. If they begin asking questions, invoke your rights immediately. The presence of law enforcement can be intimidating, and the stress of the situation can cloud judgment. Having a pre-determined strategy and understanding your rights can be the difference between navigating a difficult situation and creating further legal jeopardy.

The language used when interacting with law enforcement is also a critical component of "knowing your rights." Avoid jargon, arguments, or threats. Keep your statements concise, polite, and focused on invoking your constitutional protections. Phrases like "I am invoking my right to remain silent," and "I wish to speak with an attorney," are clear, unambiguous, and legally sound. Trying to "outsmart" an officer, engaging in lengthy explanations, or making assumptions about their knowledge of the law can be detrimental. Remember, their job is to gather information, and if you provide them with that information without legal counsel, it can and will be used against you.

Consider the scenario of a police officer asking for your identification. In most jurisdictions, if you are driving, you are required to provide your driver's license and vehicle registration. However, if you are a pedestrian and not engaged in any suspicious activity, you may not be required to provide identification unless there is a specific legal basis for the stop. If you are stopped without probable cause, and the officer asks for your ID, you can politely ask, "On what grounds are you stopping me?" If they cannot provide a legal basis, you may not be required to identify yourself. However, this can be a tricky area, and the specifics can vary by state and local ordinance. It is generally safer to provide identification if requested during a lawful stop, but understanding the basis for the stop is always your right.

The "stop and frisk" scenario, popularized by legal precedent and often depicted in media, is another area where understanding your rights is paramount. Officers can stop you if they have "reasonable suspicion" that you are involved in criminal activity. Reasonable suspicion is a lower standard than probable cause and is based on specific, observable facts that lead an officer to believe criminal activity is afoot. During such a stop, if the officer has reason to believe you are armed and dangerous, they can conduct a pat-down search of your outer clothing, known as a "frisk," to check for weapons. They cannot, however, reach into your pockets or conduct a more invasive search unless they develop probable cause during the stop. If an officer frisks you and feels something that they reasonably believe to be contraband (like drugs), they may then seize it. However, if the initial stop or the frisk itself was unlawful, any evidence found may be inadmissible in court. Again, do not resist physical contact, but clearly state your objection if you believe the stop or frisk is unwarranted.

The importance of remaining calm and collected cannot be overstated. While it is natural to feel fear or anxiety when interacting with law enforcement, allowing those emotions to dictate your response can be a disadvantage. Take a deep breath, focus on your rights, and communicate your intentions clearly and respectfully. Remember, the goal is not to win an argument, but to protect yourself legally. The justice system, for all its flaws, provides specific protections for individuals facing interaction with law enforcement. These protections are your shield. To wield them effectively, you must first know they exist and understand how to deploy them. This knowledge transforms you from a passive subject of authority into an active participant in safeguarding your own liberty and rights. It is the bedrock upon which any defense against potential injustice must be built. This understanding is not a luxury; it is a necessity in navigating the complex terrain of the American justice system.

The courtroom. The very word conjures images of hushed reverence, stern faces behind polished wood, and pronouncements that can alter the course of a life. For many, it's an alien landscape, shrouded in arcane language and bewildering procedures. It's a place where power, in its most tangible legal form, is wielded, and where the stakes can be unimaginably high. But this labyrinth, as daunting as it may seem, is not designed to be impenetrable. It is, in theory, a system built on principles of fairness and due process, a framework intended to adjudicate disputes and administer justice. Understanding its architecture, its pathways, and the players who inhabit it is not just an academic exercise; it is a vital component of reclaiming your rights, especially when you find yourself on the wrong side of a legal proceeding. Knowledge, in this arena, is not merely power; it is a lifeline.

Let's begin by demystifying some of the fundamental terms that form the bedrock of legal discourse. You'll hear about "plaintiffs" and "defendants." In civil cases, the plaintiff is the party initiating the lawsuit, the one claiming to have been wronged. The defendant is the party being sued. In criminal cases, the dynamic shifts slightly. The state, represented by a prosecutor, brings charges against the defendant, who is the individual accused of a crime. Then there are "motions." These are formal requests made to the court by one of the parties, asking the judge to make a specific ruling or take a particular action. Motions can range from simple requests to extend a deadline to complex arguments to suppress evidence. Understanding what a motion is, and that parties can actively make them, is key to grasping the proactive nature of legal defense.

The "burden of proof" is another critical concept. In criminal cases, the prosecution bears the heavy burden of proving the defendant's guilt "beyond a reasonable doubt." This is the highest legal standard, meaning the jury or judge must be firmly convinced of the defendant's guilt, with no other logical explanation for the facts presented. In civil cases, the burden of proof is typically lower, often a "preponderance of the evidence," meaning the plaintiff must show that their claim is more likely true than not true, like a scale tipping slightly in their favor. Knowing who has the burden of proof in your case immediately clarifies the strategic landscape.

The judge, of course, is the central figure in the courtroom. Often perceived as an impartial arbiter, their role is to preside over proceedings, ensure that rules are followed, interpret the law, and make rulings on legal matters. They are the gatekeepers of evidence, the deciders of motions, and, in bench trials (where there is no jury), the finders of fact. Their decisions can profoundly impact the outcome of a case. Then there are the attorneys. In a criminal case, if you cannot afford an attorney, the Sixth Amendment guarantees you the right to a public defender or court-appointed counsel. This attorney, while employed by the state, has a fiduciary duty to represent your best interests zealously. They are your advocate, your interpreter of the law, and your strategist. In civil cases, you typically must hire your own attorney, or represent yourself (pro se).

A jury is another crucial element, particularly in criminal cases and many civil cases. A jury is a group of citizens, selected from the community, tasked with listening to the evidence presented by both sides and determining the facts of the case. They then apply the law, as instructed by the judge, to those facts to reach a verdict. The process of selecting a jury, known as "voir dire," is a strategic dance where attorneys attempt to select jurors who they believe will be favorable to their case. Understanding this process, and the importance of jury selection, is essential.

Beyond the immediate courtroom drama, the judicial process unfolds through a series of stages, each with its own purpose and potential pitfalls. For criminal cases, this typically begins with an arrest. Following an arrest, you may be booked and held in jail. Within a short period, you will likely have an initial court appearance, often called an "arraignment" or "first appearance." At this stage, you are informed of the charges against you, and you will have the opportunity to enter a plea – typically not guilty, guilty, or no contest. This is also when bail is usually set, or a bond is arranged. If you plead not guilty, the case then moves forward.

One of the next critical junctures is the "preliminary hearing" or "grand jury indictment." In some jurisdictions, a preliminary hearing is held, where a judge determines if there is sufficient probable cause to believe a crime has been committed and that the defendant committed it. If probable cause is found, the case proceeds. In other jurisdictions, a grand jury, a panel of citizens, hears evidence presented by the prosecutor in secret and decides whether to issue an indictment, which formally charges the defendant. The indictment essentially signifies that the grand jury found sufficient evidence to proceed to trial.

Following indictment or a finding of probable cause, the case enters the "discovery" phase. This is a crucial period where both the prosecution and the defense exchange information and evidence. The prosecution must turn over all evidence that might be favorable to the defense, as well as evidence they intend to use at trial. The defense can also request specific information from the prosecution. This is where your attorney will be actively working to understand the state's case, identify weaknesses, and gather their own evidence. Effective discovery is paramount; it ensures that neither side is blindsided and that the trial is based on a full understanding of the facts.

After discovery, the parties may engage in "plea negotiations." It is very common for cases to be resolved through a plea bargain, where the defendant agrees to plead guilty to a lesser charge or receive a lighter sentence in exchange for avoiding a trial. Your attorney will advise you on the pros and cons of any plea offer, and the decision to accept or reject it is ultimately yours. If no plea agreement is reached, the case proceeds to trial.

The trial itself can be a complex and lengthy process. It begins with jury selection (if it's a jury trial). Then comes the opening statements, where each side outlines what they intend to prove. This is followed by the presentation of evidence. The prosecution typically goes first, calling witnesses and presenting exhibits. The defense then has the opportunity to cross-examine the prosecution's witnesses. After the prosecution rests its case, the defense may present its own witnesses and evidence. Finally, both sides deliver closing arguments, summarizing their case and urging the jury to find in their favor. The jury then deliberates and returns a verdict. If the verdict is guilty, the case proceeds to sentencing. If not guilty, the defendant is acquitted.

Even after a verdict, the judicial process doesn't always end. Appeals are a vital mechanism for challenging a conviction or sentence if there are legal errors that occurred during the trial. An appellate court does not retry the case; instead, it reviews the trial record to determine if the law was applied correctly. This can be a lengthy and complex process, often requiring specialized legal expertise.

Understanding these stages and the terminology associated with them can dramatically reduce the feeling of being adrift in a sea of legal jargon. But knowledge is not just about understanding the stages; it's also about understanding the potential leverage points and strategies available to you. For instance, the concept of "suppression of evidence" is a powerful tool. If evidence was obtained illegally – for example, through an unlawful search and seizure that violated your Fourth Amendment rights – your attorney can file a motion to suppress that evidence. If the motion is granted, the illegally obtained evidence cannot be used against you at trial, which can sometimes be enough to have charges dismissed. This highlights the critical importance of understanding your rights during interactions with law enforcement, as discussed previously.

Similarly, the "exclusionary rule" is a legal principle that prevents illegally obtained evidence from being used in court. This rule acts as a deterrent against police misconduct. If an officer violates your constitutional rights in the process of gathering evidence, that evidence may be rendered inadmissible. This is why documenting any potential violations, no matter how seemingly minor, and discussing them thoroughly with your attorney is so crucial. The chain of events, from the initial interaction with law enforcement to the courtroom, is often interconnected, and a violation at the outset can unravel the entire prosecution's case.

Consider the nuances of testimony. Eyewitness testimony, while often compelling, is notoriously unreliable. Forensic evidence, while seemingly objective, can also be misinterpreted or flawed. Your attorney's role is to scrutinize all evidence, identify its weaknesses, and present a counter-narrative if necessary. This involves understanding the scientific principles behind forensic evidence, challenging the methodologies used, and questioning the chain of custody for physical evidence. The prosecution's case is built on evidence, and undermining that evidence is a cornerstone of a strong defense.

The legal system is also replete with doctrines that can shield individuals from prosecution or conviction. For example, the concept of "mens rea," or criminal intent, is a fundamental element of most crimes. The prosecution must prove that the defendant acted with a specific mental state. If the evidence shows a lack of intent, or a mistake of fact, it can negate a key element of the crime. Defenses such as "mistake of fact," "duress," or "self-defense" all operate by challenging the prosecution's ability to prove all the necessary elements of the crime.

The power of precedent, or "stare decisis," is another fundamental aspect of the judicial system. Courts are bound by the decisions of higher courts in similar cases. This means that legal arguments are often framed by referencing past rulings. Your attorney will be adept at identifying and citing relevant case law that supports your defense. Understanding that the law is not static, but rather a body of evolving interpretations and rulings, can provide context for the arguments being made in your case.

The plea bargaining process, while efficient, also presents its own set of challenges. The pressure to accept a plea deal can be immense, especially for individuals who are indigent, overwhelmed, or simply exhausted by the legal process. It is essential to have an attorney who is willing to thoroughly explore all avenues of defense and who will not push you towards a plea simply to close a case. Your attorney's advice should be based on a realistic assessment of the evidence and the potential outcomes of a trial, not on convenience. Understanding the potential risks and benefits of a plea bargain versus going to trial is a deeply personal decision, but one that should be made with full and honest counsel.

The role of the prosecutor is also one that deserves careful consideration. While they represent the state, their ethical obligations extend beyond simply securing a conviction. They are bound to seek justice, which includes disclosing exculpatory evidence and ensuring that trials are fair. However, the adversarial nature of the system means that their primary objective is to build and present the strongest possible case against the defendant. This is why having a vigilant defense attorney is so critical – they are the counterbalance to the prosecution's power.

Even seemingly minor procedural issues can have significant consequences. For example, deadlines for filing documents, requests for continuances, and adherence to rules of evidence are all critical. A missed deadline or a procedural misstep by your attorney can severely weaken your case. This underscores the importance of finding an attorney who is not only knowledgeable about the law but also meticulous in their practice.

When you find yourself caught in the gears of the judicial system, the feeling of powerlessness can be overwhelming. The intricate dance of legal maneuvers, the formal language, and the sheer authority of the court can induce a sense of dread. But this is precisely the moment when knowledge becomes your most potent weapon. By understanding the roles of the players – the judge, the prosecutor, the defense attorney, the jury – you can better comprehend the dynamics at play. By familiarizing yourself with the stages of a case, from arrest and arraignment through discovery, trial, and potential appeals, you gain a roadmap through the labyrinth. You begin to see not just a monolithic entity of judgment, but a process with distinct steps, opportunities, and challenges.

The legal lexicon, once a barrier, can become a tool. Terms like "probable cause," "reasonable doubt," "motion to suppress," and "discovery" are not just abstract concepts; they are the building blocks of legal strategy. Knowing what they mean and how they apply to your specific situation empowers you to engage more effectively with your attorney, to ask informed questions, and to understand the advice you are given. It transforms you from a passive spectator into an active participant in your own defense. This informed participation is not merely about understanding the rules; it is about recognizing the inherent rights and protections afforded to you by the Constitution and ensuring they are upheld at every turn. The judicial process, for all its complexities, is built upon these foundational rights. Grasping them, and understanding how they are applied (or sometimes, misapplied) within the courtroom, is the first step in reclaiming your agency and navigating the system with clarity and purpose. It is the essence of transforming fear into fortitude.

The jury box. It sits at the heart of the courtroom, a raised platform where twelve ordinary citizens are sequestered, tasked with a duty as profound as any in our republic. This is not merely a collection of onlookers; this is the ultimate expression of citizen oversight within the American justice system. In an arena where the state wields immense power, the jury stands as a formidable check, a tangible representation of the people's ultimate authority in matters of guilt and innocence. They are the bulwark against unchecked governmental power, the final arbiters for many accused of crimes, and in civil disputes, they hold the scales of justice to balance competing claims. Their collective wisdom, or lack thereof, can profoundly shape individual lives and, collectively, the very fabric of our society. Understanding their role, their selection, and their potential impact is not an abstract legal curiosity; it is a crucial component of understanding how justice is, or should be, administered.

The journey to the jury box is an intricate process, often beginning with a summons delivered by mail, a stark reminder that your civic duty might call you away from your daily life to serve in this vital capacity. This summons is not a suggestion; it is a legal mandate. Those summoned form a larger group, the jury pool, from which potential jurors for specific cases are drawn. The process that follows, known as "voir dire," is far more than a mere formality. It is a carefully orchestrated examination, a probing inquiry designed to uncover potential biases and ensure that each juror can render a fair and impartial verdict based solely on the evidence presented in court. Attorneys for both the prosecution and the defense, and sometimes the judge, will question potential jurors. They probe attitudes towards law enforcement, beliefs about crime and punishment, personal experiences with the justice system, and any preconceived notions about the parties involved or the nature of the case. They are not looking for individuals with no opinions, but rather for those who can set aside personal beliefs and apply the law as instructed by the judge to the facts as they determine them to be. This selection process, while often lengthy and sometimes tedious, is critical. The composition of the jury can, and often does, determine the outcome of a trial. A juror who harbors unconscious bias, or who is unable to grasp complex legal instructions, can inadvertently skew the proceedings. Conversely, a jury composed of thoughtful, engaged individuals who are committed to their civic duty can be a powerful force for justice.

The responsibilities entrusted to a jury are immense. Once selected, they become the finders of fact. This means they are charged with listening to all the evidence – the testimony of witnesses, the presentation of physical evidence, the arguments of the attorneys – and determining what actually happened. They must sift through conflicting accounts, assess the credibility of witnesses, and piece together the narrative of events. They are not legal scholars, nor are they expected to be. Their strength lies in their connection to the community, their shared experiences, and their common sense. They are expected to apply the law, as explained to them by the judge, to the facts they have determined. The judge's instructions are paramount; they are the legal framework within which the jury must operate. However, within this framework, there lies a latent power, a capacity for a jury to reach a verdict that transcends a rigid, literal interpretation of the law.

This brings us to the concept of jury nullification. It is a controversial, yet historically significant, aspect of the jury's power. Jury nullification occurs when a jury, believing that a law is unjust or that its application in a particular case would result in an unfair outcome, acquits a defendant despite evidence that they technically violated the law. This power is not explicitly codified in law; rather, it is an inherent, unwritten prerogative of the jury system. Throughout American history, juries have, at times, used this power to resist oppressive laws, such as those that enforced slavery, prohibited alcohol, or criminalized dissent. While judges will instruct juries to follow the law as they are given it, they cannot compel a jury to convict. If a jury unanimously decides to acquit, even if the evidence seems to point towards guilt, the defendant is free. This is a profound safeguard against what might otherwise be tyrannical applications of the law. It acknowledges that justice is not always a matter of strict legal adherence, but can also involve a moral and ethical dimension.

The implications of jury nullification are far-reaching. It means that a jury, composed of everyday citizens, possesses the power to act as a conscience of the community, to refuse to enforce laws they deem fundamentally wrong. This is a potent form of citizen control over government action. It ensures that the power of the state is not absolute, that there are avenues for individual conscience to assert itself within the legal system. Of course, this power is not to be wielded lightly. Jurors are sworn to uphold the law, and disregarding it without strong moral justification can lead to unjust outcomes for victims. However, the potential for nullification serves as a vital reminder to lawmakers that their statutes must be just and humane, lest they face the resistance of a jury of their peers. It underscores the idea that the law, ultimately, derives its legitimacy from the consent and moral understanding of the people.

Consider the landmark case of

Respublica v. Weems (1795), a Pennsylvania case where a jury acquitted a man accused of piracy after finding that his actions, while technically falling under the definition of piracy, were committed under duress and were not inherently malicious. Or more famously, the acquittal of John Peter Zenger in 1735, a printer accused of libel for criticizing the colonial governor. The jury found him not guilty, effectively establishing a precedent for freedom of the press. These historical examples illustrate the jury's capacity to inject a sense of fairness and equity into legal proceedings, acting as a moral compass when the letter of the law might otherwise lead to injustice. In modern times, instances of jury nullification are often debated and rarely overtly acknowledged by courts, but the underlying power remains. It is a silent threat to potentially unjust laws, a reminder that the ultimate power to enforce those laws rests with the people.

The jury system, therefore, is more than just a mechanism for resolving disputes; it is a fundamental expression of democratic participation. It allows ordinary citizens to directly engage with the administration of justice, to hold the government accountable, and to ensure that the laws are applied in a manner that reflects the values of the community. It is a constant reminder that the power of the state is not absolute, and that the will of the people, expressed through their chosen representatives on the jury, can serve as a powerful counterweight. When you understand the jury's role – from their selection through voir dire to their ultimate deliberations and verdict – you grasp a crucial aspect of how your rights are protected, or how they can be defended, within the American legal landscape. It is in this jury box that the abstract principles of justice are brought to life, tested against the lived experiences and collective conscience of the citizenry. Their decision, whether based on strict adherence to the law or a profound sense of moral duty, is the final word in many legal battles, a testament to the enduring power of the people in shaping their own justice. The jury stands as a potent symbol of our commitment to a system where the judgment of the people, not just the dictates of the state, holds sway. This inherent power, though sometimes controversial, is a vital part of the checks and balances that define our system, a constant affirmation that justice is, at its core, a human endeavor.

The echo of the courtroom can be a deafening silence for those who find themselves on the wrong side of the law, especially when the scales of justice seem impossibly tipped against them due to a lack of resources. The American justice system, for all its ideals of fairness, can feel like an impenetrable fortress for individuals who cannot afford to hire counsel. This is a stark reality that can leave even the most innocent feeling utterly defenseless. However, the narrative does not end with this grim prospect. The system, in its imperfect design, does offer pathways for those who are financially challenged to secure the legal representation they desperately need. It's a critical part of the ongoing struggle to ensure that justice, while often expensive, is not exclusively for the privileged.

One of the most vital pillars of legal recourse for indigent defendants is the office of the public defender. These attorneys, often overworked and underpaid, are appointed by the court to represent individuals who cannot afford to hire a private lawyer. Their role is not merely to go through the motions; they are sworn officers of the court, bound by the same ethical obligations as any private attorney. They are tasked with providing a robust defense, challenging the prosecution's case, presenting mitigating evidence, and ensuring that their client's constitutional rights are protected at every stage of the legal process. The very existence of public defenders is a testament to the Sixth Amendment's guarantee of the right to counsel. Yet, the sheer volume of cases they handle can create immense pressure, making it challenging for them to dedicate the extensive time and resources that every complex case deserves. This is a systemic issue, a constant battle for resources that can, in some jurisdictions, strain the quality of representation. However, for countless individuals, the public defender is their only hope, a beacon of legal expertise in a sea of legal uncertainty. Their dedication in the face of such overwhelming odds is often the bulwark that prevents a miscarriage of justice.

Beyond the public defender system, a network of legal aid societies and non-profit organizations operates across the country, offering free or low-cost legal services to those who qualify. These organizations often focus on specific areas of law, such as housing, family law, or immigration, but many also provide assistance with criminal defense. They are often funded by a combination of government grants, private donations, and the hard work of dedicated volunteers. Legal aid societies are crucial for bridging the gap left by the public defender system, particularly in civil matters or for individuals who may not meet the strict financial eligibility for court-appointed counsel but still struggle to afford representation. These organizations often act as a safety net, catching those who might otherwise fall through the cracks. They are comprised of attorneys, paralegals, and support staff who are deeply committed to the principle that everyone, regardless of their financial standing, deserves access to justice. The work of these societies is often characterized by creative problem-solving and a deep understanding of the unique challenges faced by low-income communities. They are not just providing legal advice; they are often providing a lifeline, offering a sense of hope and empowerment to individuals facing overwhelming legal battles.

A significant avenue for obtaining legal assistance, particularly for those with complex cases or who face systemic injustices, is through

pro bono services. The term *pro bono publico*, Latin for "for the public good," refers to legal work undertaken voluntarily and without payment. Many private attorneys and law firms dedicate a portion of their practice to *pro bono* cases, recognizing their ethical responsibility to contribute to the administration of justice and to serve those who cannot afford legal services. These attorneys often bring a wealth of experience and resources to their *pro bono* clients, providing a level of advocacy that can be transformative. While *pro bono* work is invaluable, it is not always readily available for every type of case, and the demand often far exceeds the supply. Nonetheless, seeking out attorneys or firms that actively engage in *pro bono* work can be a powerful strategy for those in need of legal representation. Many bar associations maintain lists of attorneys willing to take on *pro bono* cases, and organizations dedicated to connecting *pro bono* lawyers with clients also exist. The dedication of these legal professionals, who choose to donate their time and expertise, is a profound testament to the ideal of justice for all. Their commitment not only provides essential legal support but also strengthens the fabric of our legal system by demonstrating that the pursuit of justice can transcend financial barriers.

However, the pursuit of justice does not solely rely on the availability of paid or

pro bono legal counsel. For many, becoming their own advocate, or at least an active participant in their defense, is not just an option but a necessity. This is where the concept of self-advocacy takes center stage. Understanding your rights, the legal processes involved, and the specific details of your case is paramount. While it is challenging to navigate the legal system without a lawyer, arming yourself with knowledge can make a significant difference. This involves meticulously documenting everything – conversations, documents, dates, and times. It means familiarizing yourself with relevant laws and legal procedures, even if it's at a basic level. Many courts offer self-help centers or provide information packets for individuals representing themselves, often referred to as *pro se* litigants. These resources can be invaluable in understanding the paperwork, court etiquette, and basic legal arguments. It requires courage, resilience, and an unwavering determination to be heard and understood within the legal arena. The legal system can be intimidating, but by taking an active role, individuals can ensure that their perspective is presented and that their voice, even if unrepresented by counsel, is not silenced. This process demands a deep dive into the specifics of one's case, an understanding of the evidence, and a clear articulation of one's defense. It is a demanding path, but one that empowers individuals to take control of their legal destiny when other options are unavailable.

The journey of self-advocacy can be profoundly strengthened by seeking support from advocacy groups and community organizations. These groups, often formed around specific issues or populations, provide a crucial support network for individuals navigating the legal system. They can offer emotional support, practical advice, and sometimes even connections to legal resources. For instance, organizations focused on wrongful convictions, police brutality, or prisoner rights can provide invaluable insights and guidance to individuals facing similar challenges. They often have members who have been through similar experiences and can offer firsthand knowledge and encouragement. These groups can also be powerful advocates in their own right, raising public awareness, lobbying for legislative change, and sometimes even providing limited legal support or referrals. They understand the systemic issues that can lead individuals into legal trouble and work to address those root causes. By joining forces with others who share similar struggles, individuals can amplify their voices and create a collective force for change. The power of community, in this context, cannot be overstated. It transforms isolation into solidarity, despair into determination, and individual struggles into a shared fight for justice. These organizations represent a crucial form of empowerment, reminding individuals that they are not alone and that collective action can be a potent tool in challenging an often-unforgiving system. Their work often extends beyond individual cases, aiming to reform the very systems that can entrap vulnerable populations, thereby creating a more just and equitable future for all. This collective action, while subtle in its introduction here, lays the groundwork for understanding how sustained pressure can lead to meaningful systemic change within the justice landscape.

The labyrinthine pathways of the justice system can often feel like a one-way street, leading individuals through a series of legal proceedings with little perceived recourse beyond the confines of the courtroom. Yet, the power to alter the very landscape of that system, to reshape its contours and mend its imperfections, lies not solely within the chambers of judges or the arguments of attorneys. It resides, fundamentally, with the people. The very individuals who fund this vast enterprise through their taxes, who are subject to its dictates, and who are its ultimate beneficiaries, possess a potent, often underutilized, tool: their voice, directed towards their elected representatives. Transforming from passive observers or beleaguered defendants into active architects of change requires understanding how to wield this influence effectively. It is a process that demands engagement, a commitment to civic duty that extends far beyond the ballot box, and a willingness to step into the arena of policy-making.

Reclaiming one's rights, or indeed, striving for a more equitable justice system for all, is not a solitary endeavor confined to the courtroom or the self-help legal center. It extends into the halls of power where laws are debated, budgets are allocated, and the direction of justice is charted. Elected officials, from local council members to national legislators, are the conduits through which citizen concerns can be translated into policy. They are, in theory, representatives of the people, tasked with understanding and addressing the needs of their constituents. This fundamental principle forms the bedrock of democratic governance, and its practical application is the focus of this section: building bridges to those who hold the power to enact meaningful reform. It is about more than just casting a vote every few years; it is about sustained engagement, informed advocacy, and the persistent, unwavering demand for a justice system that truly serves all. The journey from feeling powerless in the face of legal adversity to becoming an empowered agent of systemic change begins with understanding this crucial avenue of influence.

The initial step in this vital process is to identify and connect with the individuals who represent you at various levels of government. This is not an abstract concept; it is a concrete action that requires research and a willingness to reach out. At the most immediate level, there are your local representatives – city council members, county commissioners, district attorneys, and local judges. These officials often have the most direct impact on the day-to-day functioning of the justice system within your community. They are responsible for local ordinances, law enforcement policies, and the allocation of resources for courts and public defense. Understanding who these individuals are and how to contact them is paramount. Most government websites provide directories of elected officials, along with their contact information, including office addresses, phone numbers, and email addresses. Many also have staff members dedicated to constituent services, whose role is precisely to field inquiries and relay concerns to the elected official.

Reaching out to these representatives can take several forms, each with its own impact. A carefully written letter or email, detailing specific concerns about the justice system – perhaps issues with indigent defense funding, overcrowded jails, or biased policing practices – can be a powerful starting point. When composing such a message, clarity, conciseness, and a focus on actionable suggestions are key. Instead of vague complaints, articulate the problem, explain its impact, and propose a specific solution or area for investigation. For example, rather than simply stating "public defenders are overworked," one might write, "I am writing to express my concern regarding the caseloads of public defenders in our county. I understand that the average defender handles X number of cases, far exceeding recommended national standards, which I believe compromises the quality of justice. I urge you to explore options for increasing funding for public defender offices or implementing caseload limits."

A more personal touch can be achieved through telephone calls. While a brief call may not allow for the depth of detail that a written communication affords, it can convey a sense of urgency and allow for direct interaction with staff who can log your concerns. This direct human connection, even if initially with an aide, can be a valuable way to ensure your voice is heard and recorded. It's important to be prepared for these calls, to have your key points organized, and to remain polite and respectful, even if you are addressing a matter that evokes strong emotions.

For those seeking to make a more significant impact, participating in town hall meetings or public forums hosted by elected officials is an invaluable strategy. These events, often advertised through local media or government channels, provide a platform for direct engagement with your representatives in a public setting. This is an opportunity to ask questions, voice concerns, and engage in dialogue. When addressing an official in a town hall, it is crucial to be prepared. Know your issue thoroughly, be able to articulate it succinctly, and be ready to answer potential follow-up questions. Framing your question or statement in a way that highlights the impact on the community, rather than just a personal grievance, can often resonate more effectively. For instance, asking about the impact of insufficient legal aid funding on the fairness of local trials, or the effect of mandatory minimum sentencing laws on prison overcrowding and recidivism rates in your area, connects individual concerns to broader policy implications. The power of a well-posed question in a public forum can not only influence the official but also educate other attendees and spark further conversation.

Beyond direct outreach, understanding the legislative process itself is empowering. Knowing when bills are being introduced, debated, and voted upon allows you to target your advocacy efforts effectively. Many legislative bodies maintain websites that provide access to proposed legislation, committee hearing schedules, and voting records. Subscribing to email alerts from these sites can keep you informed about relevant developments. When a bill that could impact the justice system is under consideration, contacting your representatives to express your support or opposition becomes particularly potent. This can involve providing testimony at public hearings, submitting written comments, or organizing with other concerned citizens to present a united front.

The federal level offers another critical avenue for influence, particularly for issues that have national implications or require federal legislation. Your U.S. Senators and Representatives are responsible for creating federal laws, overseeing federal agencies, and allocating federal funding. The same principles of direct communication, participation in public forums, and legislative awareness apply here, albeit on a larger scale. The sheer volume of constituent requests can be overwhelming, so making your message clear, impactful, and relevant to their constituents' interests is paramount. Think about how issues like criminal justice reform, civil rights protections, or funding for legal services agencies have national reach. A coordinated effort, perhaps involving citizens from multiple states contacting their federal representatives, can create significant momentum.

The effectiveness of advocacy is often amplified when it is not a solitary voice but a chorus. Building coalitions and working with existing advocacy groups can significantly enhance your impact. Organizations dedicated to criminal justice reform, civil liberties, or specific legal rights often have established relationships with policymakers and a deep understanding of the legislative process. Joining forces with these groups can provide access to resources, expertise, and a network of like-minded individuals. Together, you can draft more comprehensive policy proposals, organize larger-scale advocacy campaigns, and present a more formidable force to policymakers. Think of the collective power of hundreds or thousands of people signing a petition, attending a rally, or flooding legislative offices with calls and letters. This demonstrates a widespread concern that elected officials cannot easily ignore.

Moreover, engaging with your representatives is not a one-time event; it is an ongoing relationship. Staying in touch, providing updates on the impact of existing policies, and continuing to advocate for reforms ensures that your concerns remain on their radar. This could involve sending follow-up letters, inviting them to visit local facilities or community centers affected by justice system policies, or simply continuing to attend town hall meetings. It's about demonstrating sustained commitment and building trust. When a representative understands that you are a thoughtful, informed constituent with a genuine interest in improving the community, they are more likely to listen and act.

The digital age has also opened new avenues for civic engagement. Social media platforms, while often a source of distraction, can be powerful tools for raising awareness and mobilizing support. Sharing information about legislative issues, organizing online campaigns, and engaging in respectful debate can reach a wider audience and put pressure on representatives to address critical concerns. Hashtags related to criminal justice reform, for instance, can become rallying points for widespread advocacy. Live-streaming town hall meetings or organizing online Q&A sessions with policymakers can also increase transparency and accountability.

However, it is crucial to approach this engagement with a strategic mindset. While passion and conviction are essential drivers, they must be coupled with pragmatism and persistence. Understanding the political landscape, the priorities of your representatives, and the potential obstacles to reform is vital. Not every initiative will succeed immediately, and some battles may be long and arduous. Yet, the act of engaging, of making your voice heard, is in itself a form of reclaiming power. It transforms individuals from subjects of the system into active participants in its evolution.

Consider the case of a community grappling with disproportionate arrests and convictions for minor drug offenses. Through research, they might discover that local ordinances or enforcement practices are contributing to this problem. Instead of passively accepting the status quo, they could organize. They might start by researching their local elected officials, identifying those on the city council or county board who have shown an interest in community safety or criminal justice issues. Then, they would begin to reach out. This could involve writing letters to the editor of the local newspaper, detailing the impact of these arrests on families and the community. They might also draft a policy proposal suggesting alternative approaches, such as diversion programs or decriminalization of certain offenses, and present it to their representatives. Attending council meetings, speaking during public comment periods, and organizing neighborhood groups to attend these meetings collectively can create a tangible presence. If a town hall is scheduled, they would prepare questions that highlight the inequities and ask for specific commitments from their representatives to review or change the problematic policies. This sustained, multi-faceted approach, demonstrating both concern and a clear vision for improvement, is how bridges are built and how the justice system can be nudged towards greater fairness.

The process of engaging with representatives is not always about grand legislative battles. It can also be about addressing specific injustices that fall within their purview. For instance, if a constituent believes their child has been unfairly treated by the juvenile justice system, they might not only seek legal counsel but also contact their local representative to highlight systemic issues that may have contributed to the outcome. This could involve sharing detailed accounts of the experience, providing evidence of potential procedural flaws, and advocating for oversight or review. In some cases, representatives can intervene by requesting information from relevant agencies or facilitating a dialogue between concerned parties and officials. While they cannot overturn court decisions, they can often play a crucial role in ensuring that due process is followed and that existing policies are applied equitably.

It's also important to understand the role of data and evidence in this advocacy. When approaching elected officials, having well-researched information to back up your claims is invaluable. This might involve collecting statistics on arrest rates, conviction disparities, sentencing patterns, or the outcomes of diversion programs. Many academic institutions, non-profit organizations, and government agencies publish reports and studies on these topics. Citing this data in your communications with representatives adds weight to your arguments and demonstrates that your concerns are grounded in evidence, not just emotion. For example, if advocating for increased funding for mental health services within the justice system, presenting data on the correlation between untreated mental illness and incarceration rates can be a persuasive tool.

Furthermore, the concept of accountability is intrinsically linked to engaging with representatives. They are elected to serve the public, and it is the public's responsibility to hold them accountable for their actions and their decisions.

This means not only communicating concerns but also tracking how representatives respond. Did they address the issue raised? Did they vote in favor of reforms? Did they allocate resources as promised? By staying informed about their voting records and public statements, constituents can make more informed decisions in future elections and continue to advocate for those who demonstrate a commitment to justice. This continuous feedback loop is essential for ensuring that elected officials remain responsive to the needs of their constituents.

Ultimately, building the bridge to your representatives is an act of civic empowerment. It is about recognizing that the systems that govern us are not immutable forces but are shaped by human decisions and public will. By actively engaging in the political process, by articulating concerns, proposing solutions, and demanding accountability, citizens can play a profound role in transforming the justice system into one that is more just, more equitable, and more responsive to the needs of all. It is a testament to the enduring power of democracy when its citizens choose to participate fully, transforming abstract rights into tangible realities.

Chapter 5: Forging a Future of Justice

The corridors of justice have long echoed with the clang of punishment, the stark pronouncements of guilt, and the unforgiving march towards retribution. For generations, our societal response to wrongdoing has been largely defined by a retributive impulse: an eye for an eye, a tooth for a tooth. Prisons, fines, and probation have served as the primary instruments, designed to isolate, deter, and, ostensibly, to serve as a cathartic release for societal outrage. Yet, beneath this veneer of order and consequence, a deeper, more insidious reality has often festered: the perpetuation of harm, the entrenchment of cycles of violence, and the profound, often irreparable, damage inflicted not only on those who transgress but also on those who have been victimized, and on the very fabric of our communities. This punitive paradigm, while deeply ingrained in our legal traditions, has proven to be a blunt instrument, often incapable of truly healing the wounds it purports to address or preventing the recurrence of the harms it seeks to punish. The evidence, mounting with each recidivist offense and each community fractured by crime, suggests a critical need for a fundamental re-evaluation of our approach. We stand at a precipice, where the limitations of purely retributive justice are becoming undeniably clear, and the call for alternative pathways, pathways that prioritize healing, understanding, and genuine repair, is growing louder.

This is where the burgeoning movement towards restorative justice offers a compelling, and dare I say, essential, counter-narrative. It proposes a radical departure from the adversarial, win-lose framework of traditional justice, inviting us instead to consider a more holistic, human-centered approach. At its core, restorative justice recognizes that crime is not merely a violation of abstract laws, but a rupture in relationships, a fracturing of community trust, and a source of profound suffering for all involved. It shifts the focus from

what law was broken? and *who broke it?* to *who has been harmed?* and *what are their needs?* and ultimately, *whose obligation is it to meet those needs?* This fundamental reframing of the problem inherently alters the potential solutions. Instead of asking how we can punish the offender, we begin to ask how we can repair the harm, restore what has been lost, and prevent future transgressions through a process of mutual understanding and accountability. It is a pathway that seeks not to simply inflict pain in response to pain, but to foster healing, reintegration, and the creation of stronger, more resilient communities. This is not a naive idealism; it is a pragmatic recognition that true justice must extend beyond the confines of the courtroom and delve into the intricate web of human connection that crime disrupts.

One of the most potent and widely recognized manifestations of restorative justice is victim-offender mediation (VOM). Imagine, for a moment, the raw courage it takes for a victim to confront the person who has caused them unimaginable pain. Imagine the profound emotional toll of recounting a traumatic experience, not to a detached panel of legal professionals, but directly to the individual who inflicted that trauma. VOM provides a carefully facilitated, structured environment where this courageous act can occur. Under the guidance of a trained, neutral mediator, victims have the opportunity to express the full impact of the crime – their fear, their anger, their grief, their sense of loss. They can ask the questions that have haunted them:

Why me? What did I do to deserve this? Will you do it again? For offenders, this process can be equally transformative. It offers a direct and unfiltered understanding of the human cost of their actions, moving beyond abstract legal consequences to confront the tangible suffering they have caused. This direct encounter with the pain they have inflicted can be a powerful catalyst for genuine remorse, empathy, and a commitment to making amends. The mediator's role is crucial; they ensure that the dialogue remains respectful, that the victim's safety and emotional well-being are paramount, and that the offender engages with sincerity and a willingness to take responsibility. The outcome of a VOM session is not a predetermined sentence, but a mutually agreed-upon plan for restitution, apology, or other actions that the victim deems necessary for their healing and for the offender to demonstrate genuine accountability. This process, when successful, can lead to a profound sense of closure for victims, reducing their fear and anger, and can foster a deep sense of responsibility and a desire for rehabilitation in offenders, thereby significantly reducing the likelihood of re-offending. It is a powerful testament to the human capacity for empathy and transformation, even in the face of profound transgression.

Beyond the direct encounter of VOM, restorative justice finds fertile ground in community-based initiatives, often referred to as circles or conferencing. These models are particularly effective in addressing offenses that have a broader impact on a community, such as vandalism, minor assaults, or disputes that strain neighborhood relations. In these settings, a wider circle of stakeholders is brought together: the victim(s), the offender(s), their families, community members, law enforcement representatives, school officials, or social workers – anyone who has been affected by or has an interest in resolving the harm. The process, often facilitated by a trained community member or a restorative justice practitioner, begins with an opening statement that sets the tone and explains the purpose of the circle: to understand what happened, to discuss who was affected and how, and to decide what needs to be done to repair the harm and prevent it from happening again. Participants often sit in a circle, a symbolic representation of equality and shared responsibility, and may pass a talking piece – an object that signifies the right to speak without interruption. This structure encourages active listening and ensures that everyone has an opportunity to share their perspective. Victims can articulate their feelings and needs, offenders can explain their actions and express remorse, and community members can voice their concerns about safety and the impact on neighborhood harmony. The collective wisdom of the circle is then harnessed to develop a plan. This might include restitution, community service, apologies, or agreements to participate in specific programs aimed at addressing underlying issues, such as anger management or substance abuse. The power of these circles lies in their ability to foster a shared sense of responsibility and ownership in resolving conflict and healing community wounds. They build social capital, strengthen relationships, and create a more resilient and supportive environment. Instead of an external authority imposing a solution, the community itself, in collaboration with those directly involved, crafts a path forward, ensuring that the resolution is not only just but also sustainable and culturally relevant. This collective approach to justice reinforces the understanding that crime is not just an individual act but a communal concern, and that the community has a vital role to play in both addressing and preventing it.

The concept of accountability within restorative justice is a nuanced and powerful one, standing in stark contrast to the often superficial nature of punishment. In a retributive system, accountability is often reduced to serving time or paying a fine – actions that can be completed mechanically, without any genuine internal shift or understanding of the harm caused. Restorative accountability, however, demands far more. It requires offenders to actively engage with the consequences of their actions, to understand the ripple effect of their choices, and to take meaningful steps to repair the damage. This might involve direct financial restitution to the victim, but it can also encompass a far broader spectrum of actions. It can mean offering a sincere and heartfelt apology, not one dictated by legal counsel, but one that emanates from a genuine understanding of the victim's pain. It can involve community service that directly benefits those affected by the offense or that addresses the underlying social conditions that may have contributed to it. It can require offenders to participate in educational programs, therapy, or support groups that help them develop better coping mechanisms, address root causes of their behavior, such as addiction or mental health issues, and build a stronger sense of self-worth. The key is that these actions are not simply penalties imposed from without, but are undertaken with a recognition of obligation and a commitment to making amends. This form of accountability fosters a deeper sense of remorse and can be a powerful motivator for lasting change. When offenders are encouraged and supported to actively repair the harm they have caused, they are more likely to internalize the lesson, to develop empathy, and to make a conscious choice to live a life that does not inflict further suffering. It is a process that respects the agency of both the victim and the offender, empowering them to be active participants in the healing and reconciliation process, rather than passive recipients of state-sanctioned penalties. This active engagement cultivates a sense of dignity and respect, even in the midst of difficult conversations, and lays the groundwork for successful reintegration into the community as a responsible and contributing member.

The potential of restorative justice to reduce recidivism is a compelling argument for its broader adoption. When individuals are processed through a system that focuses solely on punishment, the underlying issues that led them to commit offenses – be they poverty, lack of education, substance abuse, mental health challenges, or a history of trauma – often remain unaddressed. Released back into the same environments, with the stigma of a criminal record and without the necessary support systems, many find themselves trapped in a revolving door, cycling back into the justice system. Restorative justice, by contrast, aims to address these root causes. Through victim-offender mediation and community conferencing, opportunities arise to identify these underlying issues and to collaboratively develop plans for addressing them. This might involve connecting offenders with job training programs, addiction counseling, mental health services, or educational opportunities. By investing in the rehabilitation and reintegration of individuals, restorative justice seeks to break the cycle of crime and create pathways to a more constructive future. Moreover, the sense of agency and responsibility fostered through restorative processes can be incredibly empowering for individuals who have previously felt marginalized and disempowered. When they are actively involved in repairing harm and contributing positively to their communities, they begin to build self-esteem and a sense of purpose, which are crucial protective factors against future offending. The focus on building relationships and community connections, inherent in many restorative models, also provides vital social support networks that can help individuals navigate challenges and resist returning to harmful behaviors. This is not about excusing harmful actions, but about recognizing that true justice requires not only holding individuals accountable for their deeds but also investing in their capacity to become contributing members of society. The evidence, though still growing, suggests that this more holistic approach can yield significantly better outcomes in terms of reducing re-offending rates, leading to safer communities and a more humane justice system for all.

The vision of a justice system that prioritizes repair and reconciliation over retribution is not a utopian fantasy, but a tangible and achievable goal. It requires a fundamental shift in our collective mindset, a willingness to move beyond the deeply ingrained instincts of anger and vengeance, and to embrace a more compassionate and effective approach to addressing harm. This paradigm shift involves fostering a greater understanding and acceptance of restorative justice principles within our communities, legal professions, and governmental institutions. It means investing in the training and support of skilled facilitators who can guide these complex and sensitive processes. It entails developing robust evaluation mechanisms to track the effectiveness of restorative initiatives and to continuously refine their implementation. Furthermore, it necessitates a commitment to dismantling the systemic barriers that often perpetuate crime and exacerbate its impact, such as poverty, inequality, and lack of access to education and healthcare. Restorative justice is not a panacea, and it will not be suitable for every case or every individual. However, its potential to heal wounds, foster understanding, reduce recidivism, and build stronger communities is undeniable. By embracing these pathways of repair and reconciliation, we can move towards a justice system that is not only more effective in preventing crime but also more humane, more equitable, and ultimately, more just. It is a call to action, an invitation to reimagine justice not as a system of punishment, but as a process of healing and restoration, a journey towards collective well-being that benefits victims, offenders, and society as a whole. The echoes in the halls of justice can, and must, begin to resound with the promise of renewal rather than the pronouncements of perpetual retribution.

The architecture of our current justice system is, in many ways, a monument to the belief that every societal ill can, and should, be met with a criminal response. Poverty, the gnawing emptiness of hunger, the desperation born from lack of opportunity – these are not merely social conditions; in the eyes of the law, they can quickly become criminal acts. The homeless person seeking shelter in an abandoned building faces charges of trespassing. The individual struggling with addiction, driven by an overwhelming compulsion, may find themselves arrested for possession or petty theft to fund their habit. Mental illness, when it manifests in erratic behavior or perceived public nuisance, too often leads to citations, arrests, and the dehumanizing experience of being processed through the very system designed to protect, but which often further traumatizes. This pervasive criminalization of need is a self-perpetuating cycle, a testament to a fundamental misunderstanding of the nature of human suffering and societal dysfunction. It is a system that punishes the symptom while utterly ignoring the disease, treating the bark of the tree while leaving the roots to fester and spread their decay.

We must, with a profound sense of urgency and a clear-eyed understanding of the evidence, begin to dismantle this edifice of criminalization. The notion that a badge and a booking sheet are the appropriate responses to homelessness, addiction, or mental health crises is not only ineffective but morally bankrupt. These are not inherently criminal behaviors; they are indicators of profound societal failure, of communities that have not provided adequate support, of systems that have not offered sufficient care. To respond with incarceration is akin to attempting to cure a fever by locking the patient in a cold room – a punitive measure that ignores the underlying pathology and, in fact, exacerbates the condition. The individuals caught in these webs are not hardened criminals plotting malice; they are often deeply vulnerable people struggling against forces beyond their immediate control. Their circumstances demand compassion, intervention, and support, not the blunt instrument of the criminal justice system.

Consider the stark reality of poverty. When individuals lack stable housing, food security, and economic opportunity, the resulting desperation can lead to actions that are deemed illegal. Loitering, public urination, or even shoplifting essential items can become pathways into the criminal justice system. These individuals are not choosing to break the law; they are often attempting to survive in conditions that the law itself, by criminalizing survival behaviors, makes exponentially more difficult. The cost of this approach is astronomical, not just in financial terms of policing, court costs, and incarceration, but in the immeasurable human cost of lost potential, broken lives, and further marginalization. Instead of funneling resources into arresting, prosecuting, and jailing people for the 'crime' of being poor, imagine if those same resources were directed towards comprehensive affordable housing initiatives, robust job training programs, and universal access to basic necessities. This is not about excusing harmful actions; it is about recognizing that the conditions that often give rise to those actions can and must be addressed proactively, through social investment rather than punitive reaction.

Similarly, the criminalization of addiction represents a catastrophic failure of imagination and empathy. Addiction is a complex disease, a biological and psychological dependency that often stems from trauma, mental health issues, or a desperate attempt to cope with overwhelming circumstances. Yet, our default response has been to treat addiction as a moral failing, a criminal choice, leading to arrest and imprisonment for drug offenses. This approach not only fails to address the root causes of addiction but actively hinders recovery. Incarceration often isolates individuals from their support networks, exacerbates their mental health issues, and, upon release, leaves them with a criminal record that serves as a significant barrier to employment, housing, and social reintegration – all critical components of sustained sobriety. A truly public safety-oriented approach would involve a massive reallocation of resources from law enforcement and corrections towards accessible, evidence-based treatment options. This includes readily available detoxification services, long-term residential treatment programs, outpatient counseling, harm reduction strategies, and robust mental health support. When we treat addiction as a public health crisis, providing the necessary care and support, we not only foster individual recovery but also significantly reduce the crime rates often associated with the desperate behaviors driven by untreated dependency.

The pervasive issue of mental illness further highlights the absurdity and cruelty of criminalizing need. Untreated or undertreated mental health conditions can manifest in behaviors that, while sometimes disruptive or even frightening, are direct consequences of illness, not malicious intent. Individuals experiencing psychosis, severe depression, or debilitating anxiety may act in ways that lead to police intervention. Without adequate mental health infrastructure, law enforcement officers, often ill-equipped and under-trained for such situations, become the de facto first responders. This can lead to unnecessary arrests, the use of force, and the cycle of psychiatric crises being addressed within the confines of jails and prisons, facilities that are woefully inadequate for providing appropriate care and can, in fact, worsen mental health conditions. A reimagining of public safety demands a significant investment in community-based mental health services, mobile crisis intervention teams staffed by mental health professionals, and easily accessible psychiatric care. When individuals experiencing mental health emergencies receive timely and appropriate professional support, rather than the sterile, punitive environment of a holding cell, the likelihood of escalation, victimization, and recidivism is dramatically reduced. This shift represents not a softening of public safety policies, but a strategic and far more effective allocation of resources towards prevention and genuine care, thereby creating a safer society for everyone.

This radical reimagining of public safety moves beyond the traditional punitive models and embraces a philosophy of prevention and support as the primary pillars of community well-being. It acknowledges that true safety is not achieved through the accumulation of prisons and police, but through the cultivation of thriving, supportive communities. This involves a multi-faceted approach that prioritizes human needs and social determinants of health. For example, investing in high-quality, universally accessible education from early childhood through higher education is a potent crime prevention strategy. Education equips individuals with critical thinking skills, economic opportunities, and a sense of purpose, significantly reducing the likelihood of them turning to illicit activities. Similarly, ensuring access to affordable, nutritious food and safe, stable housing are fundamental to human dignity and social stability. When these basic needs are met, the desperation that can fuel crime diminishes.

Furthermore, a robust and accessible healthcare system, encompassing both physical and mental well-being, is a cornerstone of this reimagined public safety. Early intervention programs for at-risk youth, readily available counseling services, and comprehensive support for individuals recovering from addiction can prevent many of the issues that lead to criminalization. This also extends to fostering strong social connections and community engagement. Programs that encourage civic participation, create opportunities for mentorship, and build robust social support networks can significantly reduce isolation and alienation, which are often precursors to problematic behaviors. The goal is to create a society where individuals feel valued, supported, and connected, diminishing the appeal and necessity of engaging in activities that harm themselves or others.

The transition from a criminalization-first approach to one focused on prevention and support requires a fundamental reorientation of public perception and political will. It necessitates challenging the deeply ingrained narrative that equates punishment with safety. We must actively promote and fund alternatives to incarceration, such as diversion programs, restorative justice initiatives, and community-based rehabilitation services. This shift demands an honest assessment of where our public funds are being allocated and a courageous redirection of those resources towards initiatives that address the root causes of crime. It is a long-term investment, one that may not yield immediate, headline-grabbing results, but one that promises a more sustainable, humane, and ultimately safer future for all. By decriminalizing need and investing in our communities, we can begin to forge a justice system that truly reflects our values of compassion, equity, and the inherent dignity of every individual. This is not a utopian ideal; it is a pragmatic necessity for building societies that are resilient, just, and truly safe.

The chilling efficiency of the justice system, with its ironclad procedures and seemingly immutable laws, can foster a profound sense of individual powerlessness. It is easy to feel like a lone voice shouting into the void when confronting the vast machinery of the state. Yet, history, and indeed the unfolding narrative of our own times, is replete with examples that shatter this illusion. The whisper of individual discontent, when amplified and harmonized with countless others, can swell into a force capable of reshaping the very foundations of that system. This is the essence of collective action, the potent, often underestimated, engine of change that transforms passive observers into active architects of justice. It is a recognition that while one stone may barely chip away at an edifice, a thousand, a million, striking in unison, can bring down walls that once seemed impregnable.

The most fundamental, and perhaps most powerful, avenue for collective action lies in the ballot box. It is the silent thunderclap that precedes seismic shifts, the mechanism through which the collective will of the people can truly hold power accountable. Every election, from the most local school board race to the highest national office, presents an opportunity to inject our values and demands into the heart of governance. To abstain from voting is to cede that power, to allow others to define the future of justice without our input. But to engage, to educate oneself on the candidates' records, their stances on reform, and their commitment to dismantling oppressive structures, is to wield a potent weapon. It's about more than just ticking a box; it's about strategic deployment of our civic power. This involves understanding that candidates are not monolithic entities, but individuals who respond to sustained pressure and demonstrated support for specific policy changes. It requires looking beyond the superficial promises and delving into the concrete proposals. Are they advocating for robust investment in mental health and addiction treatment, or are they doubling down on punitive measures? Do their platforms champion restorative justice and community-based solutions, or do they reek of the old, failed carceral logic? Mobilizing within our communities to ensure widespread voter registration and turnout, particularly among those most affected by the failures of the current system, becomes paramount. This is not merely about electing sympathetic faces; it is about electing agents of change who are beholden to the electorate's demand for a more just and humane approach. The collective act of voting, when informed and unified, sends an unmistakable message: the status quo is no longer acceptable.

Beyond the immediate act of casting a vote, collective action manifests in the sustained, organized pressure that keeps reform on the agenda. This is where advocacy campaigns come into play, transforming individual outrage into sustained, strategic action. These campaigns can take myriad forms, from grassroots organizing that focuses on local ordinances and police accountability measures to national efforts that lobby for legislative reform at the federal level. The key is the amplification of voices. A single letter to a legislator might be filed away, but a coordinated campaign that inundates their office with thousands of letters, emails, and phone calls, all echoing the same message, cannot be ignored. Think of the painstaking work of collecting signatures for petitions, each one a small but significant endorsement of a particular reform. Imagine the power of community meetings, where neighbors gather to share their experiences, brainstorm solutions, and plan collective responses. These gatherings are not just forums for discussion; they are crucibles where solidarity is forged and action plans are born.

Peaceful protest, in its myriad expressions, serves as another vital channel for collective action, a visible and undeniable manifestation of public dissent. From silent vigils that honor victims of injustice to marches that demand systemic change, these public demonstrations capture attention, generate media coverage, and force a reckoning with uncomfortable truths. The power of a march is not solely in its numbers, but in its symbolism. It is a physical manifestation of collective will, a visual declaration that the people are united in their demand for a different future. Each placard held aloft, each chant echoing through the streets, represents a story, a grievance, a hope for a more equitable system. The careful planning, the coordination of logistics, the amplification of messages through social media and traditional outlets – these are all components of effective protest that amplify the voices of the marginalized and bring their struggles to the forefront of public consciousness. These actions, when carried out peacefully and with clear objectives, create a moral imperative for those in power to respond. They are not simply acts of disruption; they are eloquent pleas for a reevaluation of priorities and a commitment to meaningful reform.

The digital age has, in many ways, supercharged the potential for collective action. Social media platforms, once viewed primarily as tools for personal connection, have become powerful organizing hubs. Hashtag campaigns can coalesce disparate individuals around a common cause, raising awareness on a global scale. Online petitions can gather millions of signatures in a matter of days, demonstrating the breadth of public support for specific reforms. Digital tools allow for rapid dissemination of information, enabling activists to mobilize quickly in response to unfolding events or to coordinate large-scale advocacy efforts. Live-streaming protests can broadcast events to a global audience in real-time, bypassing traditional media gatekeepers and ensuring that the narratives are controlled by those experiencing injustice. This is not to suggest that digital activism is a panacea; it must be coupled with tangible, on-the-ground organizing. However, the ability to connect, mobilize, and amplify messages across geographical boundaries has fundamentally altered the landscape of collective action, making it more accessible and potentially more impactful than ever before.

Consider the power of sustained, targeted campaigns. The fight for civil rights, for instance, was not won by isolated acts of bravery, but by decades of organized effort. Boycotts that crippled businesses, sit-ins that challenged segregation in public spaces, voter registration drives that empowered marginalized communities – these were all manifestations of collective action. The legal challenges mounted by organizations like the NAACP, meticulously building cases and leveraging the courts, were a form of sustained, strategic advocacy that chipped away at discriminatory laws. This was not a spontaneous uprising; it was a deliberate, long-term strategy of collective pressure, using every available tool – legal, political, and social – to achieve its objectives.

Similarly, the movement to end mass incarceration is a testament to the evolving power of collective action. For years, the growth of the prison industrial complex went largely unchallenged, seen by many as an inevitable consequence of crime. But then, individuals began to connect their experiences. Families of incarcerated individuals shared their stories of heartbreak and injustice. Former inmates, facing immense barriers to reentry, began to organize. Academics and researchers produced data that starkly illustrated the disproportionate impact on marginalized communities and the exorbitant financial cost. This confluence of personal testimony, data-driven research, and strategic advocacy began to coalesce into a powerful movement. Organizations dedicated to criminal justice reform, many born from the very communities most impacted by the system, emerged and grew. They organized public awareness campaigns, conducted research, advocated for policy changes at all levels of government, and provided direct support to individuals and families affected by incarceration. The success of bail reform initiatives, the growing calls for sentencing reform, and the increased scrutiny of policing practices are all direct outcomes of this sustained, collective effort. What once felt like an unstoppable force is now facing a powerful, organized resistance, fueled by the collective voice of those who demand a more just and equitable future.

The narrative of forging a future of justice is inextricably linked to the story of people uniting, of individuals understanding that their personal struggles are not isolated incidents but shared experiences that demand a collective response. It is a story of transforming the quiet hum of individual frustration into a resonant chorus of demand, a symphony of action that compels the world to listen and, ultimately, to change. This is the enduring power of collective action: it is the force that reminds us that even in the face of seemingly insurmountable obstacles, the unified will of the people remains the most potent engine for justice. The path forward is not paved with individual acts of heroism alone, but with the steadfast, unwavering solidarity of a people determined to build a better tomorrow.

The echoes of past injustices, once a deafening roar, are beginning to subside, replaced by the insistent, rising tide of a new consciousness. We stand at a precipice, a pivotal moment where the accumulated weight of systemic failure compels us to question the very foundations upon which our current justice apparatus is built. For too long, this system has operated under a grim paradigm, one that has been characterized not by a pursuit of true justice, but by an adherence to an archaic model of control and punishment. This has manifested as a form of 'tyranny,' not necessarily in overt, dictatorial pronouncements, but in the insidious, pervasive ways in which it has inflicted harm, perpetuated inequality, and eroded human dignity. It is a tyranny of the inflexible rule, the dehumanizing process, and the disproportionate suffering it has inflicted, particularly upon those already marginalized and vulnerable within our society.

This paradigm of tyranny, deeply entrenched in our history, is characterized by a zero-sum approach to justice. It operates on the assumption that for one party to win, another must inherently lose, and that the state, wielding its immense power, is always positioned to be the victor. This has fostered a culture where rehabilitation is often an afterthought, where empathy is viewed as a weakness, and where the fundamental humanity of individuals, even those who have committed offenses, is frequently overlooked. The emphasis has been overwhelmingly on retribution, on isolation, and on the sterile application of statutes, often divorced from the complex realities of human behavior, social context, and the profound impact of trauma. We have built institutions designed to contain and punish, rather than to heal and reintegrate. The warehousing of individuals, often in conditions that exacerbate existing psychological and physical ailments, has become a default response, a costly and ultimately ineffective solution that perpetuates cycles of harm rather than breaking them. The pervasive 'us versus them' mentality, ingrained in the very fabric of this system, has created a chasm between those who administer justice and those who are subjected to it, a chasm that breeds mistrust and hinders any genuine path toward reconciliation or societal healing.

But the winds of change are blowing, and they carry with them the promise of a radical transformation. We are moving, collectively, towards a new covenant, one that seeks to dismantle the structures of tyranny and erect in their place a system founded on principles of justice, empathy, and love. This is not a utopian fantasy; it is a pragmatic necessity, a recognition that the current model is not only morally bankrupt but also demonstrably failing to achieve its stated objectives of safety and societal well-being. The 'new covenant' is a profound renegotiation of our relationship with justice itself, an agreement to move beyond mere critique and engage in the arduous but essential work of reimagining its purpose and its practice. It is a call to redefine what it means to be a just society, shifting the focus from vindictive punishment to restorative healing, from societal alienation to communal responsibility, and from punitive isolation to radical empathy.

This proposed covenant is built upon a tripartite foundation: mutual respect, profound accountability, and an unwavering commitment to human dignity. Mutual respect demands that we acknowledge the inherent worth of every individual, regardless of their past actions or their current circumstances. It requires us to see the person behind the offense, to understand the complex tapestry of influences that shape human behavior, and to approach every interaction with a posture of openness and a willingness to listen. This is a radical departure from a system that often strips individuals of their autonomy and their voice, reducing them to mere case files and statistics. Instead, it calls for a justice system that actively seeks to engage individuals in their own rehabilitation, empowering them to take ownership of their actions and to actively participate in their own healing and their community's restoration.

Profound accountability, a cornerstone of this new covenant, is not to be confused with the retributive impulses that have long dominated our approach. True accountability, in this framework, is about understanding the full scope of harm caused by an offense, acknowledging the impact on victims and the community, and taking meaningful steps to repair that harm. It is a process that extends beyond simple incarceration, focusing on restorative practices that encourage offenders to understand the consequences of their actions, to make amends, and to commit to living in a way that prevents future harm. This type of accountability is deeply challenging, requiring both the offender and the community to engage in difficult conversations and to confront uncomfortable truths. It necessitates a commitment from the system to provide the resources and support necessary for this restorative process to be effective, including robust opportunities for education, vocational training, mental health services, and trauma-informed care. It is about ensuring that individuals who have caused harm are held responsible not through endless cycles of punishment, but through a transformative process that fosters genuine remorse, facilitates repair, and ultimately leads to reintegration.

Central to this new covenant is an unyielding commitment to human dignity. This means recognizing that every person, by virtue of their humanity, possesses inherent worth and is entitled to fundamental rights and respect. It is about dismantling the practices that dehumanize and degrade, and instead embracing approaches that affirm the value of every life. This translates into concrete changes: eliminating solitary confinement as a form of prolonged torture, ensuring access to adequate healthcare and mental health services within correctional facilities, prohibiting the use of excessive force, and guaranteeing fair and equitable treatment for all, regardless of race, socioeconomic status, or background. It means actively working to break down the systemic biases that have historically led to disproportionate policing, sentencing, and incarceration of certain communities. Human dignity is not a privilege to be earned; it is a birthright that must be protected and upheld by the justice system.

The transition from tyranny to transformation is not merely an abstract philosophical exercise; it requires concrete, actionable solutions. It means advocating for policies that prioritize prevention and early intervention, investing in education, affordable housing, and accessible healthcare, and addressing the root causes of crime, such as poverty, addiction, and lack of opportunity. It means shifting resources away from an overreliance on incarceration and towards community-based programs that support healing, rehabilitation, and reentry. This includes expanding restorative justice initiatives, which bring together victims, offenders, and community members to collaboratively address the harm caused by crime and to find ways to repair it. It involves developing robust mental health and addiction treatment services, recognizing that many individuals who enter the justice system are struggling with complex health challenges that require compassionate care, not just punishment.

Furthermore, this transformation demands a radical reimagining of our approach to policing. It calls for a move away from militarized tactics and towards community-oriented policing models that prioritize de-escalation, relationship-building, and problem-solving. It necessitates greater accountability for misconduct, independent oversight, and a commitment to transparency. Policing should be about serving and protecting the entire community, not about occupying and surveilling it. This also extends to the court system, where we must prioritize fairness, due process, and the elimination of racial and socioeconomic disparities. This involves advocating for bail reform, sentencing reform, and the abolition of mandatory minimums that often lead to unjust and disproportionate punishments. It means ensuring that legal representation is truly adequate and accessible for all, recognizing that the quality of justice received should not be determined by the size of one's bank account.

The path forward is illuminated by the understanding that justice is not a static endpoint, but a dynamic, ongoing process of striving for a more equitable and humane society. This new covenant is an invitation to participate in that process, to embrace the discomfort of change, and to commit to building a justice system that reflects our highest aspirations. It is a call to move beyond the punitive and embrace the restorative, to replace fear with understanding, and to recognize that true safety is not achieved through isolation and punishment, but through connection, healing, and shared responsibility. This is the essence of a justice system that not only addresses harm but actively cultivates well-being, not just for those who have been harmed, but for the entire community. It is a vision where the halls of justice are not sites of fear and retribution, but spaces of healing, accountability, and ultimately, hope. This is the promise of a new covenant, a future forged in the crucible of our collective will to create a more just, compassionate, and loving world. It is a vision where the arc of justice bends not towards retribution, but towards redemption and the flourishing of every human spirit. The seeds of this transformation have been sown, and with sustained effort and unwavering commitment, they will surely blossom.

The intoxicating scent of victory, however fleeting, can lull even the most ardent revolutionaries into a dangerous complacency. We have, after all, tasted progress. The seismic shifts we have advocated for, the fundamental re-engineering of an apparatus that has long operated as a blunt instrument of oppression, are beginning to take root. The whispers of change have become a chorus, and the edifice of an outdated penal philosophy, built on the bedrock of fear and retribution, is showing fissures. But here lies the precipice, the razor's edge upon which all movements for profound societal change teeter. It is the moment after the initial battle is won, when the temptation to rest, to declare the war over, is at its strongest. This is precisely when the true work, the often-invisible, unglamorous, yet utterly vital labor of sustained vigilance, must commence.

To cease our efforts now, to allow the hard-won gains to become ossified or, worse, to be subtly dismantled by those who still cling to the old paradigms, would be to betray the very principles that propelled us forward. The architects of the former 'tyranny,' or at least its lingering beneficiaries, do not vanish with the passing of flawed legislation. They adapt, they regroup, and they wait for the moment of inattention, the opportune lull in the public's righteous anger, to reassert their influence. This is not mere cynicism; it is a sober assessment of the historical patterns that have seen reform movements ebb and flow, often leaving behind a residue of well-intentioned but ultimately hollow victories. The fight for justice is not a sprint, but an unrelenting marathon, demanding an endurance that can sometimes feel more arduous than the initial charge.

The 'tyranny tax' is a concept that we must keep alive, not just as a historical marker of what we have overcome, but as a constant reminder of the insidious ways in which injustice continues to extract its toll. This is not a literal monetary levy, but the immeasurable cost levied upon individuals, families, and entire communities by a system that prioritizes punishment over rehabilitation, exclusion over integration, and fear over understanding. It is the generational impact of mass incarceration, the stifled potential of individuals denied opportunity due to a criminal record, the erosion of trust between law enforcement and the communities they are meant to serve, and the profound psychological wounds inflicted by punitive measures that often exacerbate rather than address the underlying issues. Abolishing this 'tyranny tax' requires more than just legislative reform; it demands a fundamental cultural shift in how we perceive crime, culpability, and redemption. It requires us to actively dismantle the systems that perpetuate this tax and to build, in its stead, pathways to healing and genuine societal repair.

The 'watchful citizen' is the essential bulwark against the re-emergence of these harmful systems. This is not a call to arms in the literal sense, but a profound appeal to an informed, engaged, and persistent citizenry. It is the individual who refuses to let the news cycle dictate their commitment, the person who understands that legislative victories are merely the opening of a door, not the final destination. This 'watchful citizen' is the parent who educates their children about the nuances of the justice system, the neighbor who advocates for community-based rehabilitation programs, the student who engages in critical dialogue, and the retired professional who lends their expertise to oversight committees. They are the quiet guardians, the steadfast advocates who ensure that the principles of the new covenant are not merely etched in stone but are actively lived and breathed in the everyday functioning of our society.

Consider the implementation of restorative justice practices. The passage of laws mandating or encouraging such programs is a monumental step. However, the true measure of their success lies not in their existence, but in their execution. Are these programs adequately funded? Are they staffed by trained facilitators capable of navigating complex emotional landscapes? Are victims truly empowered to participate in a process that respects their needs and experiences? Are offenders being held to a standard of accountability that fosters genuine remorse and facilitates meaningful amends? The watchful citizen asks these questions. They attend community meetings, they monitor the allocation of resources, and they speak out when they witness the dilution or perversion of these vital initiatives. Without this persistent oversight, restorative justice risks becoming another bureaucratic checkbox, a well-intentioned policy gathering dust on a shelf, rather than the transformative force it is intended to be.

The commitment to 'justice without love's absence' is the ultimate aspiration, and the watchful citizen is its most ardent protector. 'Love,' in this context, is not a sentimental ideal but a profound recognition of shared humanity, an empathetic understanding of the complexities that lead to harm, and a commitment to healing and reconciliation. It is the antithesis of the cold, detached, and often cruel calculus that characterized the previous era of punitive justice. It means recognizing that individuals caught within the gears of the justice system, even those who have caused significant harm, are still human beings deserving of dignity and capable of change.

This translates into a constant questioning of the systems that dehumanize. Are correctional facilities environments that foster rehabilitation and personal growth, or are they incubators of despair and further alienation? Are the conditions of confinement humane, providing adequate healthcare, educational opportunities, and avenues for meaningful connection? The watchful citizen demands transparency. They advocate for independent oversight, for access to facilities, and for the abolition of practices that serve only to break the human spirit, such as prolonged solitary confinement. They understand that a system that inflicts gratuitous suffering cannot truly be called just.

Furthermore, 'justice without love's absence' requires us to challenge the narratives that demonize and dehumanize. The media, often driven by sensationalism, can perpetuate stereotypes and fear-mongering, painting individuals with broad strokes of criminality and irredeemability. The watchful citizen actively counters these narratives. They seek out diverse perspectives, they share stories of transformation and redemption, and they challenge the simplistic 'us versus them' dichotomy that the old system so effectively exploited. They understand that fostering empathy and understanding is as crucial to achieving a just society as any legislative reform.

The journey from a system of tyranny to one of genuine justice is not a single event, but an ongoing process of cultivation and care. It requires us to be gardeners of our societal well-being, constantly tending to the fragile shoots of progress, weeding out the persistent tendrils of injustice, and ensuring that the soil of our communities is rich with the nutrients of equity, compassion, and accountability. The 'watchful citizen' is the dedicated gardener, armed with knowledge, fueled by conviction, and committed to the long, rewarding work of nurturing a future where justice truly flourishes, a future where the 'tyranny tax' is not just abolished, but forgotten, and where justice is not merely an abstract concept, but a lived reality, infused with the undeniable presence of love and humanity.

The fight extends into the subtlest of policy shifts. For example, changes in sentencing guidelines, even those intended to be more equitable, can be subtly undermined by judicial discretion that subtly favors punitive outcomes. The watchful citizen remains informed about these shifts, scrutinizing court decisions, and advocating for clearer, more consistently applied standards. They understand that the language of reform can be co-opted by those who wish to maintain the status quo, dressing old practices in new clothes. This vigilance requires a commitment to continuous learning, to staying abreast of legal developments, and to engaging in the often-tedious work of policy analysis. It is the willingness to dive into the bureaucratic weeds, to understand the mechanics of the system, and to identify the points of potential slippage.

Moreover, the concept of "accountability" itself is a fertile ground for subtle regression. In the old paradigm, accountability was primarily punitive. Now, we strive for profound accountability, which includes repair and reintegration. However, without diligent oversight, the emphasis can easily drift back towards punishment. Are the restorative justice programs genuinely facilitating repair, or are they merely a less punitive form of punishment? Are the opportunities for education and vocational training within correctional facilities truly robust and geared towards meaningful employment, or are they superficial offerings that fail to equip individuals for successful reentry? The watchful citizen asks these questions, not to obstruct progress, but to ensure that progress is genuine and effective. They advocate for metrics that measure not just recidivism rates, but also the successful reintegration of individuals into their communities, their ability to secure stable employment, and their contribution to society.

The impact of historical injustices, particularly those rooted in racial and socioeconomic disparities, cannot be erased by a single legislative act. The systemic biases that were embedded within the old justice system have a long and tenacious life. They manifest in implicit biases that can influence prosecutorial decisions, jury deliberations, and judicial sentencing, even among those who genuinely believe they are acting impartially. The watchful citizen is acutely aware of this insidious legacy. They advocate for ongoing diversity and inclusion training for all actors within the justice system, from law enforcement officers to judges and parole board members. They support initiatives that promote data collection and analysis to identify and address racial disparities at every stage of the legal process. They understand that true justice requires a proactive and continuous effort to dismantle the enduring structures of inequality.

The role of advocacy groups and community organizations cannot be overstated in sustaining this movement. These entities often serve as the frontline sentinels, diligently monitoring the implementation of reforms, providing essential services to those impacted by the justice system, and acting as a vital communication channel between the public and the institutions of justice. The watchful citizen supports these organizations, whether through financial contributions, volunteer work, or by amplifying their messages. They recognize that collective action, coordinated by these experienced groups, is often more effective than isolated efforts. These organizations are the institutional memory of the movement, the repositories of lessons learned, and the agile forces that can mobilize quickly when existing protections are threatened.

Furthermore, the watchful citizen understands the interconnectedness of justice with other societal issues. They recognize that factors such as poverty, lack of affordable housing, inadequate access to mental healthcare and addiction services, and systemic educational inequalities are root causes that contribute to crime. Therefore, their vigilance extends beyond the confines of the courthouse or the correctional facility. They advocate for policies that address these broader social determinants of crime, understanding that a truly just society is one that prevents harm by fostering well-being and opportunity for all its members. This holistic approach is essential to ensuring that the 'tyranny tax' is not merely shifted to a different domain, but truly abolished.

The journey towards 'justice without love's absence' is a continuous evolution. It requires us to be open to new insights, to adapt our strategies as circumstances change, and to remain steadfast in our core principles. The watchful citizen embraces this dynamism. They understand that the work is never truly finished, that each victory, however significant, is a stepping stone, not a final destination. They are the living embodiment of the movement's commitment to progress, the unwavering guardians of a future where justice is not a privilege for the few, but a fundamental right for all, a future where the echoes of tyranny are silenced by the sustained chorus of engaged citizenship and the enduring presence of human compassion. This is the enduring legacy we must strive to create, a testament to our collective capacity for change and our unwavering belief in the possibility of a more just and humane world.

Back Matter

Accountability (Profound): Beyond mere punishment, accountability encompasses acknowledgment of harm, sincere remorse, and active efforts towards repair and reintegration into the community.

Criminal Justice Reform: Efforts aimed at modifying laws, policies, and practices within the justice system to ensure greater fairness, equity, and effectiveness.

Incarceration (Mass): The phenomenon of a disproportionately high number of individuals being imprisoned within a society, often linked to social and economic disparities.

Justice without Love's Absence: A justice system that, while upholding accountability and consequences, fundamentally recognizes and respects the inherent humanity and dignity of all individuals, fostering empathy and the potential for redemption.

Restorative Justice: A philosophy and practice of justice that focuses on repairing harm and addressing the needs of victims, offenders, and communities, often through dialogue and mediation.

"Tyranny Tax": The immeasurable, ongoing cost levied upon individuals, families, and communities by punitive and oppressive justice systems, encompassing lost potential, generational trauma, erosion of trust, and psychological damage.

Watchful Citizen: An informed, engaged, and persistent member of society who actively monitors the justice system, advocates for progressive reforms, and ensures that hard-won gains are not eroded.

Alexander, M. (2010). *The New Jim Crow: Mass Incarceration in the Age of Colorblindness*. The New Press.

Bostrom, N. (2014). *Superintelligence: Paths, Dangers, Strategies*. Oxford University Press.

Braithwaite, J. (1989). *Crime, Shame, and Reintegration*. Cambridge University Press.

Davis, A. Y. (2003). *Are Prisons Obsolete?* Seven Stories Press.

Dobbs, L. (2020). *The Justice Delusion: How Our Legal System Fails the Innocent*. Skyhorse Publishing.

Ferrell, J. O., Hayward, S. W., & Morash, M. J. (2016). *Crime and Punishment: Sociological Foundations*. SAGE Publications.

Freire, P. (2000). *Pedagogy of the Oppressed*. Continuum.

Gottschalk, M. (2015). *Caught: The Prison State and the Crisis of American Masculinity*. Basic Books.

Harris, A. (2008). *From the War on Poverty to the War on Crime: The Making of Mass Incarceration in America*. Hill and Wang.

Kendi, I. X. (2016). *Stamped from the Beginning: The Definitive History of Racist Ideas in America*. Nation Books.

Loftus, E. F. (2005). *Eyewitness Testimony*. Harvard University Press.

Mauer, M., & Young, R. (2015). *The Meaning of Life: Reflections of Prisoners*. The Sentencing Project.

Rothstein, R. (2017). *The Color of Law: A Forgotten History of How Our Government Segregated America*. W. W. Norton & Company.

Shalev, C. (2002). *Crime and Transcarceration*. Oxford University Press.

Silberman, M. (1978). *The Political Economy of Sentencing. British Journal of Criminology, 18*(4), 352-361.

Simon, J. (2001). *Driving Down Crime: Realism about the Impact of Prisons. The Public Interest, 143*, 59-71.

West, C. (1993). *Race Matters*. Beacon Press.

Williams, B. (1985). *Ethics and the Limits of Philosophy*. Harvard University Press.

www.ingramcontent.com/pod-product-compliance
Lightning Source LLC
LaVergne TN
LVHW082358200926
848481LV00012B/3602
* 9 7 9 8 2 3 2 9 4 6 3 1 9 *